101 LINEBACKER DRILLS

Jerry Sandusky
Cedric X. Bryant

COACHES CHOICE

ISBN: 1-57167-087-4
Library of Congress Catalog Card Number: 96-72470

Book Layout: Michelle Summers
            Antonio J. Perez
Diagrams: Michelle Dressen
Cover Design: Deborah M. Bellaire
Front and Back Cover Photos: Bill Pegram

Coaches Choice Books is an imprint of: Sagamore Publishing, Inc.
                                           P.O. Box 647
                                           Champaign, IL 61824-0647
                                           (800) 327-5557
                                           (217) 359-5940
                                           Fax: (217) 359-5975
                                           Web Site: http//www.sagamorepub.com

DEDICATION

To the Penn State football players—past, present, and future:

*Many of America's finest young men,
excelling through hard work and a resolute
commitment to excellence.*

ACKNOWLEDGMENTS

The authors are grateful to the many individuals at Sagamore Publishing who provided professional assistance of the highest level. We would also like to express our appreciation to Roseanne Cowles for her invaluable typing assistance.

CONTENTS

Chapters

Mission

The Second Mile challenges young people to achieve their potential as individuals and community members by providing opportunities for them to develop positive life skills and self-esteem, as well as providing education and support for parents and professionals addressing the needs of youth.

Perspectives

The Second Mile provides a network of prevention, early intervention, and community-based child development programs and services that are provided free to school-aged children throughout Pennsylvania. The Second Mile's programs range in scope from providing exposure to strategies and skills effective in addressing problems of normal development encountered by children in the mainstream to programs and services for children who have been battered and abused, lack parental encouragement and role modeling, or who lack the skills necessary to cope with the trauma and crises confronting their families. Each program focuses on instilling a sense of personal responsibility and preparation for the future in the youngsters.

History

The Second Mile was founded by Jerry Sandusky, the assistant head football coach and defensive coordinator for Penn State University. Through his leadership and the support of many community members, the organization, which was founded and incorporated in 1977, began program operations in 1982. Initially, program services were provided to 45 children in the State College area. Today, more than 100,000 children participate in eight early intervention, prevention, and community-based programs. Hundreds of teachers, school counselors, human service professionals and families refer children to the programs annually.

Early Intervention Programs

Summer Challenge Camp Program. The goal of the Summer Challenge Camps is to provide an environment in which youngsters 8-13 years of age can begin to develop a better understanding of themselves and others. The activities focus upon building the self-awareness and confidence of campers and teaching them to work cooperatively with their peers. All campers are identified by school counselors or youth service workers as needing additional support and guidance.

During the camp experience, youngsters are asked to identify areas in which they would like to improve during the ensuing school year. If they make significant progress toward achieving their goals, they earn a return trip to camp.

In an effort to provide a continuous program of support for these young people throughout their adolescence, the *SMILE (Second Mile Intensive Learning Experience) Program* was developed. Open to campers beyond the age of the regular camp program, SMILE continues to build cooperation, self-esteem, and confidence as participants choose to explore areas, such as career development, leadership, or outdoor education.

Whether they participate in the camps or SMILE, youngsters receive year-round support from The Second Mile.

Friend Program. Weekends are special to many children and adults who may go bowling, swimming or ice skating, or just sit around and spend time together. These people participate in the Friend Program of the Second Mile. The heart of the Friend Program is the hundreds of student volunteers from the Penn State campus, including members of sports teams, fraternities, sororities, and interest houses. For many of those College Friends, befriending a Young Friend away from home is a tremendous buffer against homesickness. What the program offers these Young Friends is an opportunity to build their self-esteem, as well as an environment in which they can learn to interact with other children and adults.

Prevention Programs

Nittany Lion Tips. Recognizing that youngsters often look to athletes for their role models, The Second Mile created Nittany Lion Tips, sports trading cards highlighting exceptional Penn State student-athletes speaking to youth about the problems of normal development. Each card pictures an athlete and includes a brief biography. Most importantly, it features a message of encouragement from the player about such issues as peer pressure, school achievement, and community involvement. Available to elementary, middle, and junior high school students across the state through their school counselors and principals, the Tips are one way these professionals reinforce behavior change, reward positive behavior and establish rapport with youngsters in need of support.

Coach Jerry Sandusky and a young participant in the highly successful Second Mile Program.

PEAK. The path toward adulthood is not smooth and straight: along the way, all youngsters experience some inevitable "bends," or disappointments, and encounter many "forks," or choices which have to be made. The PEAK Program (Prevention, Education and Awareness for Kids) is a series of videotaped vignettes which highlight issues of normal development, such as dealing with peer pressure, with disappointment, and with feelings of rejection. The program offers children the opportunity to explore difficult issues, to share feelings, and to rehearse coping strategies with adult guidance in the company of their classmates. The first module, "Choice of Champions," introduces former prominent Penn State athletes who share mistakes that they made in dealing with peer pressure and strategies for avoiding similar mistakes.

Community-Based Programs

Foster Family Support. There are some very special people in Pennsylvania—foster parents. These are individuals, who like Jerry and Dottle Sandusky, have opened their homes and hearts to children with special needs. Foster parents offer friendship, love, and security to support children who are often confused and frightened about their life circumstances.

In addition to helping County Children and Youth Service Agencies recruit foster parents through the creation of public service announcements, The Second Mile acknowledges the contributions of these extraordinary people and supports their efforts through organized foster family activities. These activities, such as picnics and trips to recreational parks, provide excellent opportunities for interaction and support among foster parents, as well as a special time for family sharing.

A Better Chance Program. Since 1988, talented and motivated minority students from inner-city and poor learning environments have had the chance to leave their areas and attend State College schools through the "A Better Chance" (ABC) Program, a national organization which helps gifted minority youth achieve a brighter future through education and career guidance. The students are selected from a nationwide pool of applicants by both the Program Committee of The Second Mile and the staff at the ABC's Boston headquarters. They're housed at a Second Mile residence, where houseparents and tutors work with them during the school year. Area families serve as hosts for these students, providing them with social and emotional support, the opportunity for recreation and the chance to become better acquainted with the State College community.

CHAPTER 1

WARM-UP DRILLS

DRILL #1: HIGH KNEE RUNNING IN PLACE

Objective: To warm up; to loosen up the hips and legs.

Equipment Needed: None.

Description: Linebackers spread out in three lines with the lines spaced five yards apart. On command, the linebackers run in place at half speed. Special emphasis is placed on having the players lift their knees at least as high as their waists. Their arms are held up at approximately a 90-degree angle. The coach can subsequently have the players either speed up or slow down the speed at which they're running in place as desired.

Coaching Points:

- Linebackers can loosen up their shoulders by swinging their arms in a full circle as they run in place.

- Variety can be added to the drill by having the linebackers run forward or backward at various speeds (while continuing to lift their knees high) on command by the coach.

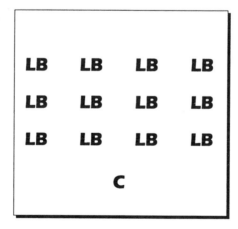

DRILL #2: HIGH KNEE CROSSOVER

Objective: To warm up; to loosen the hips and legs; to develop the hip rotator muscles; to improve footwork.

Equipment Needed: None.

Description: Linebackers spread out in three groups on the marked chalk lines of the field. The linebackers should turn and face the chalk line. On command, the linebackers run forward at half speed while lifting their knees at least as high as their waists. As they run, linebackers rotate their hips and alternately step on the opposite side of the chalk line.

Coaching Points:

•   The coach can vary the speed at which the linebackers are required to run.

•   Special emphasis should be placed on having the linebackers keep their heads up while running with their knees lifted high.

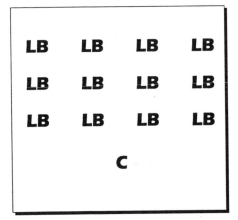

DRILL #3: CARIOKA

Objective: To warm up; to loosen up the hips, legs, and waist.

Equipment Needed: None.

Description: The coach has the linebackers spread out in front of him. On command, the linebackers run sideways, alternately placing one foot in front and one foot in back. The linebackers run from sideline to sideline.

Coaching Points:

- Variety can be added to the drill by having the coach toss a football to the linebackers. Such an action will help improve both hand skills and reaction time. The ball should be thrown at or below the linebacker's waist.

- Linebackers should be reminded to keep their hips flexed.

```
LB  LB  LB  LB  LB  LB

LB  LB  LB  LB  LB  LB

            C
```

DRILL #4: DUCK WADDLE

Objective: To warm up; to loosen up the hips and knees; to develop lower body muscular endurance.

Equipment Needed: None.

Description: The coach has the linebackers spread out in front of him. The linebackers should assume a stance that involves an exaggerated level of flexion in their hips and knees (i.e., like a duck). On command, the linebackers move forward and backward at half speed, while maintaining their flexed "duck-like" body position.

Coaching Points:

- Linebackers should be encouraged to stay off their heels while participating in the drill.

- The coach should emphasize to the linebackers that they should keep their heads, arms, and pads in a game-like position during the drill.

```
LB  LB  LB  LB  LB  LB

LB  LB  LB  LB  LB  LB

            C
```

DRILL #5: LATERAL SLIDE

Objective: To warm up; to improve the ability to move laterally.

Equipment Needed: None.

Description: The coach has the linebackers spread out in one or more lines facing him. Using a hand signal, the coach directs the linebackers to laterally slide one step in the direction he points. They then come to a complete stop and assume their proper defensive stance. Next, the coach again signals for the linebackers to laterally slide one step either in the same or the opposite direction. After a predetermined number of slides, the coach then points straight ahead to signal the linebackers to sprint as fast as they can past him.

Coaching Points:

• The drill can be modified to require the linebackers to continue to slide laterally until told to stop before they assume their defensive stance.

• The coach should emphasize that the linebackers should maintain proper body position at all times during the drill.

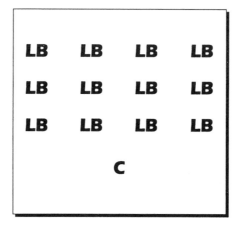

DRILL #6: SEAT ROLL

Objective: To warm up; to develop the ability to quickly get off the ground in proper body position.

Equipment Needed: None.

Description: The linebackers spread out and line up facing the coach. The linebackers then assume a good movement position. On command from the coach (e.g., "ready"), the players drop to the ground, quickly roll over on their hips, and recover to the up (e.g., starting) position. The coach visually signals to the linebackers whether they should roll left or right. After a set number of repetitions, the coach gives the command "go" and the linebackers sprint past him.

Coaching Points:

- This drill is appropriate for all defensive players.

- The linebackers should keep their heads up and their eyes focused on the coach while rolling on their hips.

LB LB LB LB LB LB

LB LB LB LB LB LB

C

DRILL #7: MOVE-STOP

Objective: To warm up; to improve reaction time; to enhance stamina.

Equipment Needed: A football.

Description: The coach has the linebackers spread out in several lines facing him. Each linebacker should be at least double-arms length from the closest player to him. With the ball in hand, the coach moves the ball in one of four directions (left, right, forward and backward). The linebackers respond to the movement of the ball and move in the direction indicated by the coach.

Coaching Points:

•   The coach should require his linebackers to respond to a new command every four to five seconds.

•   Proper alignment and stance should be stressed at all times.

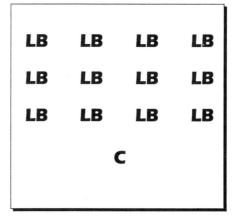

CHAPTER 2

BASIC STANCE/ MOVEMENT DRILLS

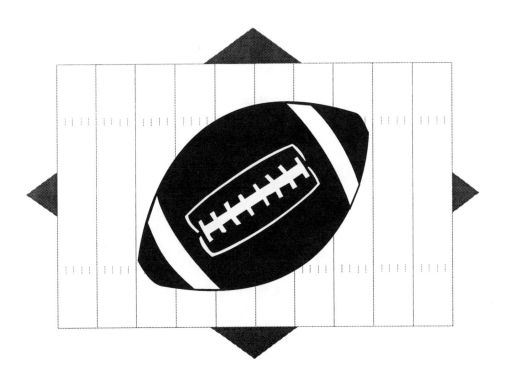

DRILL #8: ON COMMAND POSITION

Objective: To teach linebackers to assume a good defensive stance.

Equipment Needed: None.

Description: The coach has the linebackers spread out in one or more lines facing him. On command from the coach, the linebackers assume a proper defensive stance. The coach then reviews a list of general guidelines concerning what constitutes a proper stance and makes sure that the players have responded appropriately. This list should include the following:

- The linebacker's feet should be shoulder width apart or slightly wider.
- The linebacker's toes should be pointed straight forward.
- The weight of the linebacker's body should be on the toes and the balls of his feet, but his heels should not be off the ground.
- The linebacker's knees should be bent and positioned slightly beyond his feet.
- The linebacker's legs should be tense (i.e., muscles contracted) and ready to undertake a sudden movement.
- The linebacker's hands should be positioned slightly outside his knee joint with his palms facing inward and parallel to his leg.
- The linebacker's neck should be bulled (i.e., tensed) with his eyes looking up at the target.
- The linebacker's upper body should be relaxed in order to facilitate ease of movement, but should become tense immediately before contact.

Coaching Points:

- Proper alignment and stance should be stressed at all times.

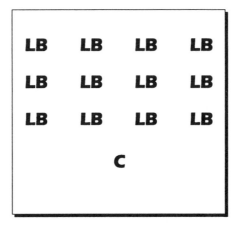

DRILL #9: STANCE WALK

Objective: To teach linebackers to maintain a good defensive stance while walking in different directions.

Equipment Needed: None.

Description: The coach has the linebackers spread out in one or more lines facing him. On command from the coach, the linebackers assume a proper defensive stance and walk in different directions, while maintaining a good hitting position (refer to Drill #8 for general guidelines concerning a proper defensive stance).

Coaching Points:

• Proper alignment and stance should be stressed at all times.

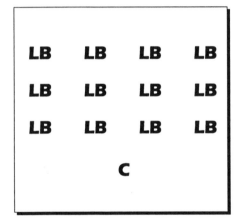

DRILL #10: STANCE RUN

Objective: To teach linebackers to maintain a good defensive stance while running in different directions.

Equipment Needed: None.

Description: The coach has the linebackers spread out in one or more lines facing him. On command from the coach, the linebackers assume a proper defensive stance and run in different directions, while maintaining a good hitting position (refer to Drill #8 for general guidelines concerning a proper defensive stance).

Coaching Points:

•   Proper alignment and stance should be stressed at all times.

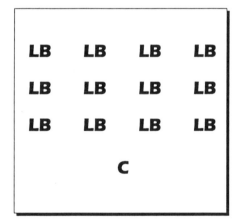

DRILL #11: SPRINT-GATHER

Objective: To teach linebackers to maintain a good defensive stance while sprinting forward.

Equipment Needed: A football.

Description: The coach has the linebackers spread out in one or more lines facing him. On command from the coach, the linebackers should sprint forward at full speed, then gather themselves, coming under control in a good hitting position.

Coaching Points:

* The importance of linebackers being able to come under control in a good hitting position after sprinting should be stressed.

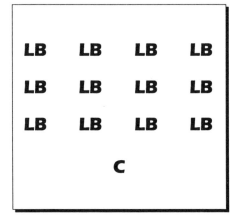

DRILL #12: QUICK FEET

Objective: To develop quick moving feet; to improve the ability of a linebacker to react and move laterally while maintaining a good movement position.

Equipment Needed: None.

Description: The linebackers spread out and line up facing the coach. They assume a good movement position—their head erect, their back flat, their shoulders square, a slight bend at the knees and waist, their arms hanging loosely in front of their bodies, and their weight supported on the balls of their feet. On command from the coach (e.g., "ready"), each linebacker starts moving his feet quickly in place. The coach then gives a directional signal (clenched fists together with his thumbs flashing the direction he wants the players to move laterally). After several change of directions laterally, the coach then gives a command (e.g., "ready, ready") that requires the linebackers to reassume their starting positions, quick moving feet, etc. After repeating the pattern several times, the coach yells out a command (e.g., "go") that requires the linebackers to sprint past him.

Coaching Points:

• This drill is appropriate for all defensive players.

• Emphasis should be placed on action-reaction, proper body position, proper body movement, and quickness.

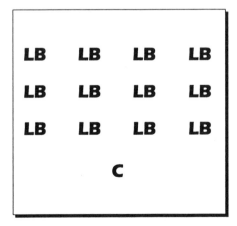

DRILL #13: QUARTER EAGLE

Objective: To warm up; to develop the ability to open and close the hips quickly; to improve reaction time; to improve footwork.

Equipment Needed: None.

Description: The linebackers spread out and line up facing the coach. They assume a good movement position—their head erect, their back flat, their shoulders square, a slight bend at the knees and waist, their arms hanging loosely in front of their bodies, and their weight supported on the balls of their feet. On command from the coach (e.g., "ready"), each linebacker starts moving his feet quickly in place. The basic step in the drill involves requiring the linebackers to turn their feet and hips, first one way and then the other. The coach has the option of giving the linebackers four different movement hand signals: (turn) left, (turn) right, up, and down. If the signal is up, the linebackers must jump up and swing their arms overhead. If the signal is down, each linebacker quickly drops to the ground (hitting his chest) and then recovers to the starting (i.e., up) position. After a sufficient number of movements, the coach commands "go," which is a signal to the linebackers to do a forward roll and sprint past the coach.

Coaching Points:

•	While in the up position, the linebackers should remain in a good movement position with their feet moving in short, choppy steps.

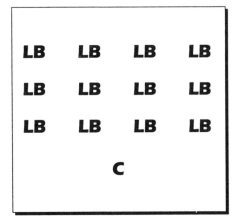

DRILL #14: LATERAL START

Objective: To teach linebackers the proper techniques for initiating lateral movement.

Equipment Needed: None.

Description: The coach has the linebackers stand in a straight line facing him. With a hand signal, the coach directs them to slide once in the direction that he points and then come to a complete stop, while maintaining their stance. He then repeats a signal for them to move one slide step in the same or opposite direction. After a number of slides, the coach points straight ahead, and the players turn and run full speed in a straight line for a distance of five yards, looking back over their shoulders at the coach.

Coaching Points:

• A proper warm-up should precede this drill.

• The linebackers should be instructed to maintain a good hitting position at all times during the drill.

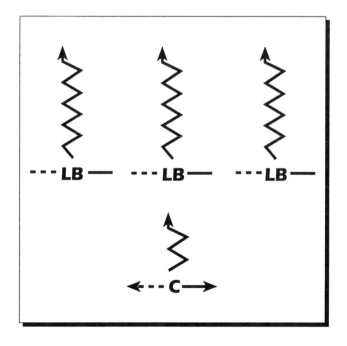

DRILL #15: CONTINUAL SLIDING (SHUFFLING)

Objective: To teach linebackers the proper techniques for sustaining lateral movement.

Equipment Needed: None.

Description: The drill is organized in the same manner as the lateral start drill (refer to Drill #14). The difference between the drills is that when the coach signals to one side, the players continue to slide in that direction until the coach gives them a signal to stop (all the while maintaining a good stance). The coach then gives a signal to slide in the opposite direction. After a number of direction changes, the coach signals, and the players sprint in a straight line for a distance of five yards, looking back over their shoulders at the coach.

Coaching Points:

- A proper warm-up should precede the drill.

- The linebackers should be required to maintain a good hitting position at all times during the drill.

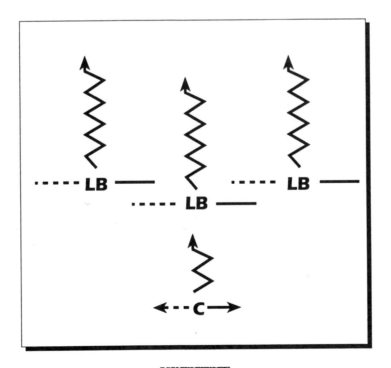

DRILL #16: LATERAL RUN (CROSSOVER)

Objective: To teach linebackers the proper techniques for running laterally.

Equipment Needed: None.

Description: The drill is organized in the same manner as the lateral start drill (refer to Drill #14). The difference between the drills is that when the coach signals to one side, the linebackers run laterally in that direction, keeping their shoulders square and using a crossover step, instead of sliding. The coach then gives a signal to run in the opposite direction. After a number of direction changes, the coach signals, and the linebackers sprint in the same manner as they did at the conclusion of the lateral start drill.

Coaching Points:

- A proper warm-up should precede the drill.

- The linebackers should be instructed to maintain a good hitting position at all times during the drill.

- The linebackers should be reminded to never cross their feet while moving laterally.

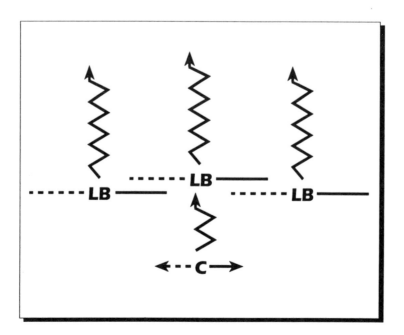

DRILL #17: MIRROR CROSSFIELD

Objective: To train linebackers to mirror a ball carrier while moving laterally.

Equipment Needed: A football.

Description: The drill starts with a ballcarrier (BC) who walks or sprints in a straight line, changing from one speed to another. He should stay at one speed for at least five yards. When the ballcarrier gets to a marker (twenty-five to thirty yards away), he steps forward to either side. The linebacker (LB) mirrors the ballcarrier by sliding or running laterally, staying slightly behind him, and maintaining the same distance between them (approximately two yards). He stays lateral until the ballcarrier turns up, and then he tackles him. If conducted without pads, the drill is ended with a "push-acceleration." In this instance, the linebacker places his hands on the ballcarrier's shoulders (instead of tackling him), extends his arms, and attempts to push the ballcarrier back.

Coaching Points:

•	Proper tackling techniques should be emphasized.

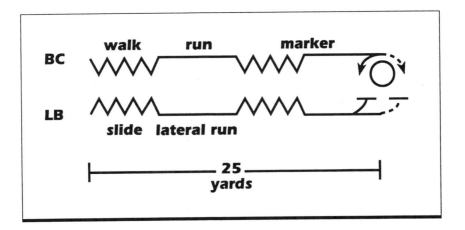

DRILL #18: CHANGE OF DIRECTION RACE (LATERAL RACE)

Objective: To evaluate and improve a linebacker's ability to quickly change directions.

Equipment Needed: None.

Description: The linebackers stand facing the coach with their near foot on a line. On a hand signal from the coach, they run laterally, keeping their shoulders square to the coach until they touch or cross a line of five yards five times (a total distance of twenty-five yards). They then repeat the drill facing in the opposite direction.

Coaching Points:

•   A proper warm-up should precede the drill.

•   The linebackers should be instructed to maintain a good hitting position at all times during the drill.

•   The linebackers should be reminded to never cross their feet while moving.

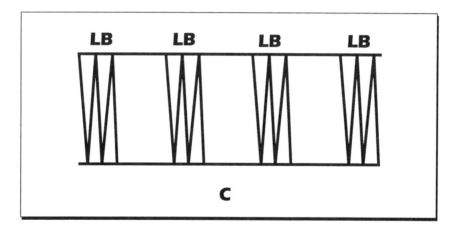

DRILL #19: CHANGE OF DIRECTION RACE
(FORWARD-BACKWARD RACE)

Objective: To evaluate and improve a linebacker's ability to quickly change directions.

Equipment Needed: None.

Description: The linebackers stand with both feet behind the line and their shoulders parallel to the line. On a signal from the coach, they sprint forward five yards until they touch or cross the next line. Then, they run backwards to the starting line and repeat the sequence until they have gone five times (a total of twenty-five yards).

Coaching Points:

· A proper warm-up should precede the drill.

· The linebackers should be instructed to maintain a good hitting position at all times during the drill.

· The linebackers should be reminded to never cross their feet while moving.

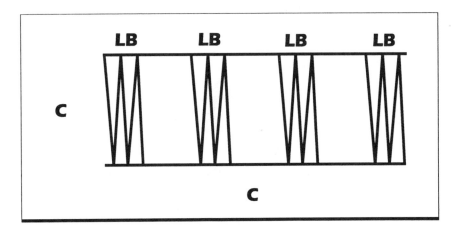

DRILL #20: AROUND-THE-BAG

Objective: To develop a linebacker's quickness; to teach a linebacker to strain into pressure without becoming overextended and to recover by making a second effort.

Equipment Needed: A large, blocking bag.

Description: The ballcarrier (BC) stands at one end of a blocking bag that is lying on the ground, while the linebacker stands at the other end and faces the leader. The ballcarrier comes forward on one side of the bag and steps into the linebacker. The linebacker reacts by coming forward on that side of the bag and pushes the ballcarrier back a short distance, maintaining his head high with his buttocks lowered to prevent overextension, his back arched, and his feet accelerating with short, choppy steps. Both men recover and race to the other side of the bag and repeat the same procedure. On the last contact (usually the third), the linebacker strains and pushes the ballcarrier back beyond the bag.

Coaching Points:

- The linebackers should be instructed to keep their heads high with their buttocks lowered to prevent overextension upon contact.

- Emphasis should be placed on proper body position, proper body movement, and quickness.

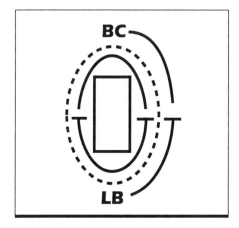

DRILL #21: LATERAL FILL AROUND-THE-BAGS

Objective: To develop a linebacker's quickness; to teach a linebacker to strain into pressure without becoming overextended and to recover by making a second effort.

Equipment Needed: Four or more large, blocking bags.

Description: Four or more bags are placed on the ground so that they are parallel to each other. The drill is executed in the same manner as the around-the-bag drill (refer to Drill #20) except that after each contact, both the ballcarrier (BC) and the linebacker (LB) continue on to the next alley. The linebacker pushes the ballcarrier back beyond the bag after they have gone around the last bag.

Coaching Points:

• The linebackers should be instructed to keep their heads high with their buttocks lowered to prevent overextension upon contact.

• Emphasis should be placed on proper body position, proper body movement, and quickness.

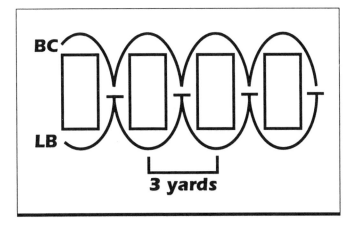

DRILL #22: DIAMOND MIRROR

Objective: To develop the ability of linebackers to change directions on both the signal of a coach and the action of an opponent while running either backwards or laterally.

Equipment Needed: None.

Description: To begin the drill, the linebackers position themselves as diagrammed, facing the coach. The coach first signals the closest linebacker to him to run either backwards in a straight line, laterally at forty-five degree angles, or forward in a straight line. The other three linebackers do what the first man does, trying to maintain the same distance between each other. On a final signal from the coach, everyone sprints full speed past the coach.

Coaching Points:

- Emphasis should be placed on proper body position, proper body movement, and quickness.

- The drill is designed to enable linebackers to respond to two stimuli simultaneously.

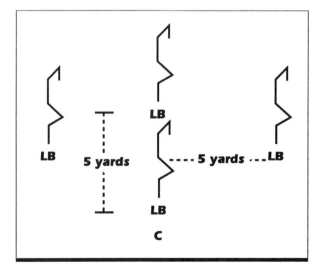

DRILL #23: MIRROR DODGE (SCORE)

Objective: To develop quickness; to practice sliding; to enhance the ability of a linebacker to react to an offensive player without becoming overextended. It also provides an excellent tool to evaluate the movement ability of a linebacker.

Equipment Needed: Two large blocking bags.

Description: The ballcarrier (BC) stands about three to four yards from a line between two long bags lying on the ground. He attempts to cross the line between the two bags as fast as possible by moving laterally and faking the linebacker (LB) who is mirroring him. As soon as the ballcarrier crosses the line, he returns to the starting position and tries to score (by crossing the lines untouched) as many times as possible in a given time limit, usually fifteen to twenty seconds. The linebacker slides to stay in front of the ballcarrier, trying to prevent him from scoring. While the linebacker may use his hands, the emphasis is on moving the feet and not being overextended. To emphasize the importance of moving the feet, the drill is done occasionally with the linebacker putting his hands behind his back.

Coaching Points:

- The linebackers must not be permitted to overextend their arms while using their hands on the ballcarrier.

- To emphasize the need for a linebacker to move his feet, the drill can be performed by requiring the linebacker to keep his hands behind his back during the drill.

- The ballcarrier should be given a specific time limit (e.g., 15 seconds) in which to score.

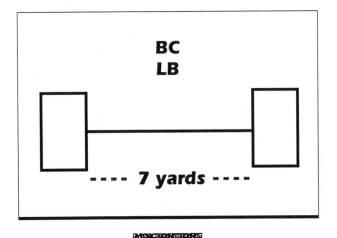

DRILL #24: PROPER PURSUIT

Objective: To teach and practice the proper angles of pursuit and how to converge on the ball.

Equipment Needed: One football.

Description: The drill involves nine players—five designated offensive players (two receivers, two running backs, and a quarterback) and four linebackers. The offense has three plays it runs at the defense. The defense must react to each play, pursue the ball, and touch the offensive player with the ball. Initially, each play is walked through by all players. After a few times, all plays are run at full speed. The first play involves a simple down-the-line option play where the quarterback (QB) runs along the line of scrimmage and pitches the ball to the nearest running back (RB). The second play involves having the quarterback drop back and throw a flare pass to a running back. On the third play, the quarterback throws the ball to one of the wide receivers (WR).

Coaching Points:

- As the linebackers touch the ballcarrier, they should practice using the up and under technique to develop the ability to strip the ball loose.

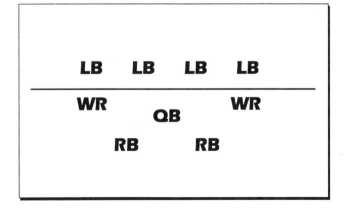

DRILL #25: ANGLE PURSUIT

Objective: To teach the linebackers the proper angles of pursuit.

Equipment Needed: Five large blocking dummies and two footballs.

Description: Five large blocking dummies are placed one yard apart on a 45-degree angle and perpendicular to a selected line of scrimmage (LOS). A row of linebackers (LB) are positioned adjacent to the first blocking dummy. On the coach's command, the first linebacker steps forward and assumes a good defensive stance next to the row of blocking dummies. He then begins to shuffle over and through the blocking dummies. At some point during the shuffle, the coach tosses a football to the linebacker. The linebacker catches the football, tucks it under his arm, and continues shuffling over the row of blocking dummies. The drill should be conducted until all of the linebackers have had a sufficient number of repetitions.

Coaching Points:

- The drill should also be conducted with the angle of the blocking dummies reversed.

- The linebackers should be encouraged to maintain a good defensive stance throughout the drill.

- The linebackers should be required to pump their arms and legs as they move over and through the blocking dummies.

- The linebackers should be instructed not to use crossover steps.

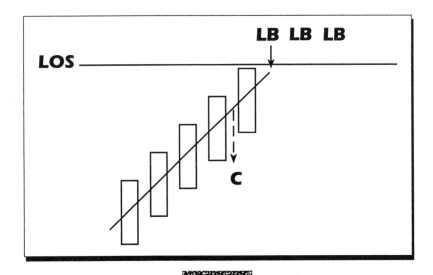

DRILL #26: SKELETON PURSUIT

Objective: To teach linebackers the proper angles of pursuit and the proper way to converge on the ball.

Equipment Needed: A football.

Description: The coach or quarterback (QB), two running backs (RB), and two wide receivers (WR) run three plays at the linebackers (LB). Each play is first walked through, including the defensive pursuit lanes, then is run at full speed. The first play is a simple down-the-line option where the quarterback comes along the line of scrimmage and pitches the ball to the nearer back. The ballcarrier runs for the sideline, then turns toward the goal-line. All linebackers must take the proper lane of pursuit and touch the ballcarrier. Next, the quarterback drops back and throws a flare pass to one of the backs. The ballcarrier heads for the goal-line, and the linebackers converge and touch him. Finally, the quarterback throws the ball out to one of the wide receivers, and the linebackers pursue and touch the runner.

Coaching Points:

- The linebackers should be required to maintain a good defensive stance throughout the drill.

- The linebackers should be instructed not to use crossover steps while moving.

- All linebackers should be encouraged to sprint to the ball carrier.

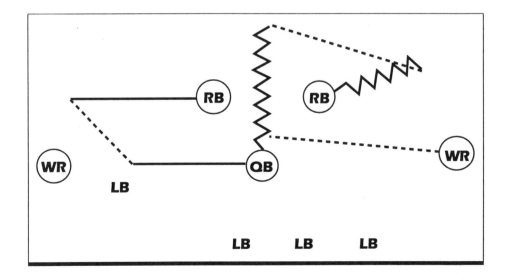

DRILL #27: BETWEEN THE BAGS

Objective: To improve a linebacker's ability to change directions quickly while moving laterally.

Equipment Needed: A minimum of four blocking bags.

Description: The blocking bags are placed on the ground parallel to each other as illustrated in the diagram. The coach (C) assumes a position at one end of the row of blocking bags. The linebacker (LB) begins in a position just outside to the left of the first bag, facing toward the coach. On a signal from the coach, the linebacker slides or runs laterally between the blocking dummies at approximately a 45-degree angle. When he reaches the outside of the next blocking dummy, the linebacker pivots back to the inside (while continuing to face the coach). The drill continues non-stop in the same manner. After the linebacker reaches the last blocking bag, he sprints backwards for five yards at full speed.

Coaching Points:

- Competition can be added to the drill by having groups of players compete against each other in relay fashion.

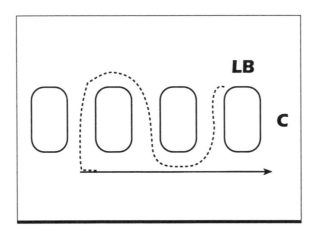

DRILL #28: LOOKING BACK

Objective: To develop a linebacker's ability to run with his shoulders turned and looking back.

Equipment Needed: None.

Description: The linebackers (LB) spread out and line up facing the coach (C). On command from the coach (e.g., "ready"), the linebackers do a quarter-turn left, while keeping their eyes focused on the coach. They then start their feet moving in place, using quick choppy steps. The coach next gives the command "move" which is a signal to the linebackers to run 20 yards backwards with their shoulders and hips turned 90 degrees. On this leg of the drill, the linebackers use a crossover step— left foot over right. After running 20 yards, the linebackers turn around and sprint back to the original starting line. The drill is repeated. This next leg of the drill is performed by the linebackers using a right-over-left crossover step.

Coaching Points:

• Linebackers should "pump" their arms as they run backwards.

• The linebackers should be instructed to keep their eyes focused on the coach.

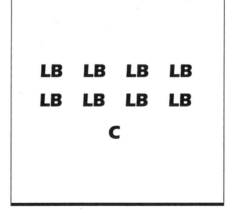

DRILL #29: OVER THE BODIES

Objective: To develop the ability of a linebacker to quickly change direction, to move laterally over simulated bodies, and to pick up his feet when he's moving.

Equipment Needed: Four or more blocking bags.

Description: The linebackers line up in two lines, behind four blocking bags which have been placed side-by-side approximately four to five yards apart. The first linebacker in each line steps up to the left side of the bag and assumes a good movement position. On command from the coach (e.g., "ready"), both linebackers start moving their feet quickly in place. The coach then gives a directional signal to start the two linebackers moving laterally over the blocking bags. The linebackers continue moving back and forth over the bags until the coach commands "ready position," which is a signal to the linebackers to reassume the starting position. At that point, the coach can either continue the drill or command "go" to have linebackers sprint past him.

Coaching Points:

- The linebackers should remain low with their shoulders facing straight ahead while performing the drill, and cross over the blocking bags with the foot closest to the bag.

- Emphasis should be placed on proper body position, proper body movement, and quickness.

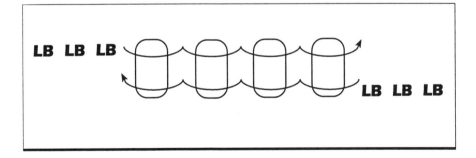

DRILL #30: HIP TWISTER

Objective: To teach a linebacker to stay low, open his hips, and keep his shoulders square, while moving laterally.

Equipment Needed: None.

Description: The linebackers spread out and line up facing the coach. They assume a good movement position—head erect, back flat, shoulders square, a slight bend at the knees and waist, their arms hanging loosely in front of their bodies, and their weight supported on the balls of their feet. On command from the coach (e.g., "ready"), each linebacker starts moving his feet quickly in place. On command from the coach (e.g., "go"), each linebacker extends his arms laterally and runs laterally in a crossover fashion. For example, if he is running left, he puts his right foot in front and then his right foot behind. The drill continues until the coach either commands "ready position" to have the linebackers reassume their starting positions or "go" to require the linebackers to turn and sprint past him.

Coaching Points:

• Speed is not essential in this drill.

• The coach should emphasize that each linebacker should stay low, keep his shoulders square, and perform his crossover steps in an exaggerated fashion (i.e., turn his belly button to the front and then to the rear, etc.).

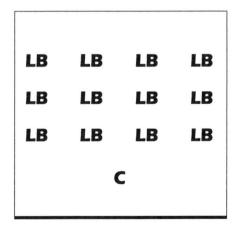

CHAPTER 3

TACKLING DRILLS

DRILL #31: FORM TACKLING (FIT)

Objective: To teach linebackers the proper form for making a tackle.

Equipment Needed: None.

Description: The linebackers spread out in lines facing the coach. On command from the coach, the linebackers practice the fit phase of form tackling. The linebacker is fitted into the ballcarrier in the proper contact position. The linebacker's knees should be bent. His hips should be lower then those of the ballcarrier. His back should be straight with his head up and his neck bowed. His eyes should be focused on the jersey number of the ballcarrier.

Coaching Points:

- This drill should be performed in just a walk-through fashion; it should never be performed live against a ballcarrier.

- The relationship between using proper techniques while tackling and the safety of the tackler should be emphasized.

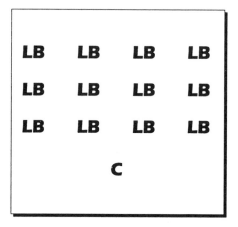

DRILL #32: FORM TACKLING (FIT AND FOLLOW THROUGH)

Objective: To teach linebackers the proper form in making a tackle.

Equipment Needed: None.

Description: From the fitted position (refer to Drill #31), the linebacker drives through the ballcarrier, wrapping his arms, keeping his head up, and accelerating his feet. The linebacker should pick the ballcarrier up and carry him backwards for approximately five yards (or until the coach blows his whistle).

Coaching Points:

- This drill should be performed in just a walk-through fashion; it should never be performed live against a ballcarrier.

- The relationship between using proper techniques while tackling and the safety of the tackler should be emphasized.

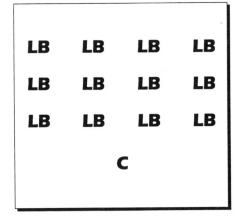

DRILL #33: BAG TACKLING

Objective: To teach linebackers the proper form in making a tackle.

Equipment Needed: Two upright dummies.

Description: Two upright dummies are positioned five yards apart, with the coach in between them, several yards away. One at a time, but in rapid succession, a linebacker sprints from the coach's left (or right), squares off facing him, and then reacts to the coach's hand signal. The coach holds the linebacker in position momentarily, then quickly points to one of the upright dummies to his right or left. The linebacker watches the coach, pumps his feet, then sprints and tackles the bag indicated by the coach. In the meantime, the next linebacker has already sprinted to a position opposite the coach, awaiting his hand signal.

Coaching Points:

- The coach may shuffle and head fake, etc., before he signals to the linebacker which dummy to tackle.

- The linebacker should set up in a good hitting position, until the coach indicates which bag should be tackled.

- The proper fundamentals and techniques of tackling should be stressed.

- The linebacker should work right, left, and diagonally with his head up, while coming toward the coach.

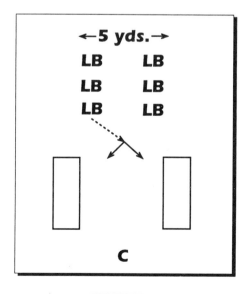

DRILL #34: EXPLOSIVE TACKLING

Objective: To teach and practice using the proper form in tackling; to develop explosiveness in tackling.

Equipment Needed: A sled.

Description: This drill involves teaching tackling in a step-by-step, progressive fashion. The linebackers line up in front of the sled (in as many lines as there are stations on the sled). On command from the coach, the drill begins by having the linebackers assume a proper contact position (for tackling) against the sled. This position is the one they should be in when initially making contact with a ballcarrier. From this initial contact position, the linebackers next drive through the sled, wrapping their arms around the sled station, keeping their heads up and their feet moving. They keep driving through the sled until the coach blows his whistle. Finally, the linebackers—starting from a good hitting position approximately three yards from the sled—fire into the sled at full speed, simulate making a proper tackle, and follow through until the coach stops play.

Coaching Points:

* The relationship between form and safety should be emphasized.

* Proper body position and proper tackling techniques should be required during all steps of the drill.

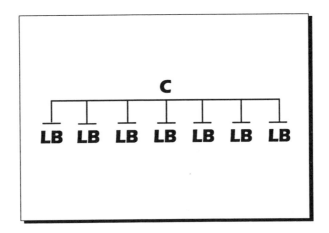

DRILL #35: ATTACK-A-BAG

Objective: To force the linebacker to move and change directions before making a tackle.

Equipment Needed: Two blocking bags.

Description: Two bags are positioned about eight yards apart with a coach (or a player) standing in the middle between the bags. A linebacker is positioned 10-12 yards away from the bags. The linebacker moves forward as fast as possible, yet in good position. When he reaches a point approximately five yards from the bags, the coach steps to one side or the other. The linebacker then angles toward that bag, drives his head across in front of the bag, turns into the bag, picks it up, and takes it back five yards. When practicing without pads, tackling is simulated with a push-acceleration (i.e., the linebacker places both hands under the ballcarrier's shoulders, with his head up, his back arched, and his feet moving in short, choppy steps).

Coaching Points:

- The proper fundamentals and techniques of tackling should be stressed.

- The linebaker should work right, left, and diagonally with his head up, while coming toward the coach.

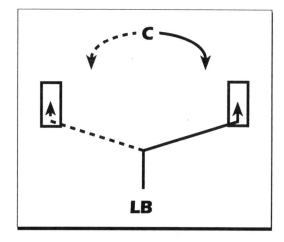

DRILL #36: ONE-ON-ONE DIVE

Objective: To enhance the ability of a linebacker to play off various types of blocks and make a tackle.

Equipment Needed: Two blocking bags; a football.

Description: Two bags are laid on the ground parallel to each other approximately five yards apart. An offensive blocker is positioned between the bags, while a ballcarrier sets up about five yards directly behind him. The linebacker aligns facing the blocker. The coach signals for the blocker either to fire straight ahead or to execute a low block to one side. If the coach points straight ahead, the ballcarrier goes to either side of the blocker, but stays inside the bags. The offensive blocker then gets involved in the drill. The linebacker plays off the block and makes a tackle.

Coaching Points:

- The proper techniques in taking on and shedding the blocker should be stressed.

- The proper fundamentals and techniques of tackling should be emphasized.

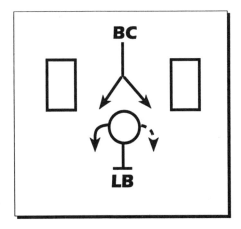

DRILL #37: TWO-ON-TWO DIVE

Objective: To enhance the ability of a linebacker learn to play off various types of blocks and make a tackle.

Equipment Needed: Four blocking bags; a football.

Description: The drill is organized in the same way as the dive drill, except that two additional bags are positioned about three yards outside the other bags, and that there are two blockers and two linebackers involved. The coach signals the type of blocks (same as in the dive drill) and the starting count. The coach calls the starting signals. If the blockers go straight ahead, the ballcarrier runs forward and stays within the inside bags. If the blockers attempt to block the linebacker to one side, the ballcarrier goes between the two outside bags in the other direction. The linebackers play the blocks and make the tackle whichever way the ballcarrier chooses to run.

Coaching Points:

- The proper techniques in taking on and shedding the blocker should be stressed.

- The proper fundamentals and techniques of tackling should be emphasized.

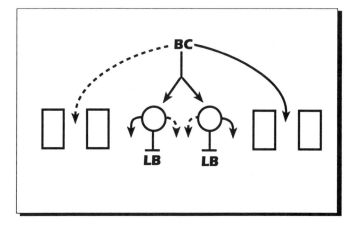

DRILL #38: SCORE TACKLING

Objective: To force the linebacker to move and change directions before making a tackle.

Equipment Needed: Three or more large blocking bags; a football.

Description: Three to five bags are positioned on the ground parallel to each other about two yards apart. The ballcarrier and the linebacker align on opposite sides of the middle bag. The ballcarrier runs back and forth between the outside bags and tries to fake the linebacker. On the command "score," the ballcarrier runs straight up the nearest alley. When the command is given, the ballcarrier tries to get across the far front edge of the bags. The linebacker mirrors the ballcarrier and attempts to tackle the ballcarrier and drive him back before he crosses the front edge of the bags.

Coaching Points:

- The relationship between using proper techniques while tackling and the safety of the tackler should be emphasized.

- The ballcarrier should be given a specific time limit (e.g., 15 seconds) in which to score.

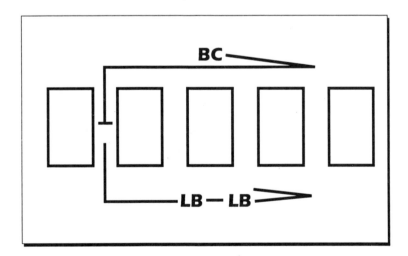

DRILL #39: THREE-ON-ONE KEY

Objective: To enhance the ability of a linebacker react to a key, play off various types of blocks, and make a tackle.

Equipment Needed: Two blocking bags; a football.

Description: Two bags are laid on the ground parallel to each other, about seven yards apart. Three offensive blockers (O) are positioned alongside each other in a three- or four-point stance, between the bags. A ballcarrier aligns himself approximately five yards behind the middle blocker. The linebacker starts opposite the middle blocker. The coach signals to one of the blockers and initiates the action with the command "go." If he points to one of the outside blockers, that blocker comes at an angle and blocks the linebacker above the waist. The ballcarrier breaks in that direction and stays inside the bags. The linebacker slides, plays the block, and makes the tackle. If the coach points to the middle blocker, he also gives him a direction. On command, the blocker tries to gain position on that side and to block the linebacker below the waist. The ballcarrier goes to that side and runs between the bag and the outside blocker. The linebacker plays off the block and makes the tackle.

Coaching Points:

- The proper techniques in taking on and shedding the blocker should be stressed.

- The proper fundamentals and techniques of tackling should be emphasized.

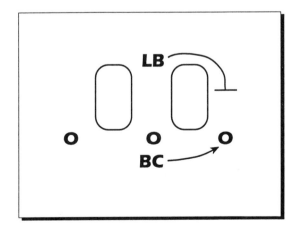

DRILL #40: INSIDE LINEBACKER KEY

Objective: To enhance the ability of an inside linebacker to play off blocks and make a tackle after moving laterally.

Equipment Needed: Three blocking bags; a football.

Description: Three bags are laid on the ground parallel to each other, about three yards apart. A blocker is positioned in a three- or four-point stance in each of the two alleys. A ballcarrier is positioned about three yards on the opposite side of the middle bag. The coach signals to one side and initiates the action with the command "go." On the command, the ballcarrier starts to the signaled side, while the blocker comes forward and high blocks the linebacker. The ballcarrier breaks anywhere between the two bags. The linebacker slides in the direction of the ballcarrier, plays the block, and makes the tackle.

Coaching Points:

- The proper techniques in taking on and shedding the blocker should be stressed.

- The proper fundamentals and techniques of tackling should be emphasized.

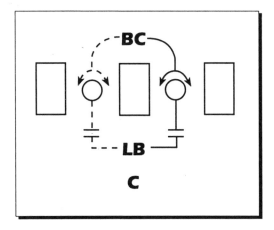

DRILL #41: ON-THE-RUN SLED

Objective: To teach and practice proper tackling in the open field.

Equipment Needed: A one-player sled.

Description: The linebackers line up in a single file, approximately seven to nine yards in front of the sled in a good, ready football position. On command from the coach, the first linebacker in line sprints toward the sled with his body under control. Keeping his eyes on the middle of the sled pad (or the numbers of the ballcarrier if a player-versus-player format is used), the linebacker tackles the sled, explodes up and through the sled, wraps his arms around it, and drives it backwards in a straight line for several yards.

Coaching Points:

- The linebacker should sprint to the sled, while keeping a proper base and maintaining good body control.

- The linebacker should hit the sled pad with his shoulders square and his legs underneath him.

- The linebacker can use an under-and-up arm action while tackling to practice stripping the ball.

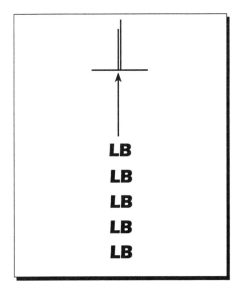

DRILL #42: BLAST THE BAG

Objective: To teach and practice the proper techniques for tackling.

Equipment Needed: A blocking/tackling bag.

Description: The drill involves two players at a time. One holds the bag upright; the other tackles the bag using proper form. The two players line up approximately three yards from each other. On command, the linebacker, moving at half speed, tackles the bag using proper techniques at all times. As the drill progresses, the linebackers gradually increase the speed at which they perform the drill until they run it at full speed.

Coaching Points:

- The linebacker should keep his head up and his eyes focused on the center of the bag while moving toward the bag.

- The linebacker should drive into the middle of the bag, explode up and through the bag, and lock his arms around the bag upon contact. Upon contact, the linebacker should keep his legs moving and attempt to drive the bag backwards.

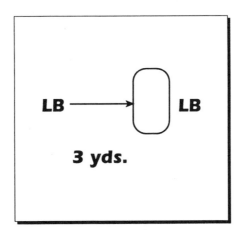

DRILL #43: MIRROR TACKLING

Objective: To practice proper tackling techniques; to develop footwork and the ability to take a proper pursuit angle.

Equipment Needed: One football; two blocking dummies.

Description: The drill requires placing the two dummies in a standing position on a yard line approximately ten yards apart. Each dummy is held by a player. Two players at a time are actively involved in the drill. One acts as a ballcarrier, while the other serves as the tackler (linebacker). The two participants start the drill facing each other about ten yards apart in the middle between the two dummies. On the initial command by the coach, the ballcarrier runs left and right several times—all the while maintaining the five-yard separation from the yard line on which the dummies were placed. The linebacker mirrors the ballcarrier while also keeping his initial distance from the yard line. On the next command from the coach, the ballcarrier explodes toward one of the dummies. The linebacker sprints toward the same dummy, running at an angle which would enable him to tackle the ballcarrier at the location of the dummy. Instead, the linebacker tackles the dummy, which is supported by a teammate.

Coaching Points:

- By taking the proper angle, the linebacker should arrive at the dummy at the same time as the ballcarrier.

- The player holding the dummy should offer resistance (i.e., by pushing forward as the linebacker explodes into it) against the linebacker.

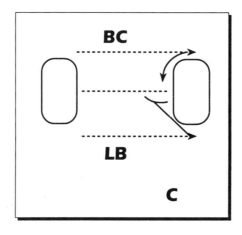

DRILL #44: SUPINE TACKLING

Objective: To enhance the ability of a linebacker to get up off the ground and to execute the proper techniques and fundamentals of tackling.

Equipment Needed: Two blocking bags; a football.

Description: The linebacker lies in a supine position on his back with the top of his helmet touching the front line of a five-yard square. The football is placed five yards away at the back line of the square, at the heels of the ballcarrier, who is facing away from the linebacker. On the coach's command, the ballcarrier must whirl around, pick up the football, attempt to evade the linebacker, and advance to the opposite side of the square. The linebacker, in turn, must roll over quickly on the same command, spring to his feet, get in a good hitting position, and tackle the ballcarrier. The blocking bags are stationed three yards apart so the ball carrier has a limited area in which to evade the linebacker.

Coaching Points:

•   The linebacker should be required to spring to his feet (in a good hitting position) as quickly as possible.

•   The proper fundamentals of tackling should be stressed.

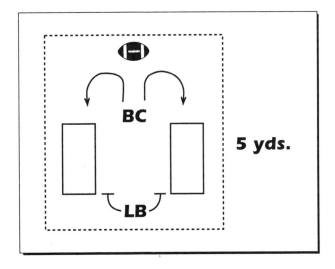

DRILL #45: ANGLE TACKLING

Objective: To teach linebackers to tackle properly after sprinting toward a ballcarrier; to practice maintaining body control prior to tackling after sprinting.

Equipment Needed: A football.

Description: The drill involves two players—each approximately ten yards away from a yard line. One acts as a ballcarrier, while the other is designated as a tackler (linebacker). On command from the coach, the ballcarrier and the linebacker sprint toward each other. When the ballcarrier reaches the yard line, he cuts left or right at a 90-degree angle. The linebacker runs as fast as he can straight ahead for seven yards, comes to a stop under control approximately three yards from the ballcarrier, reacts to the actions of the ballcarrier, and makes the tackle.

Coaching Points:

- The linebacker should maintain a good base and keep his feet moving prior to making the tackle.

- Proper form and tackling techniques should be emphasized.

- The linebacker should try to keep the ballcarrier from crossing the yard line.

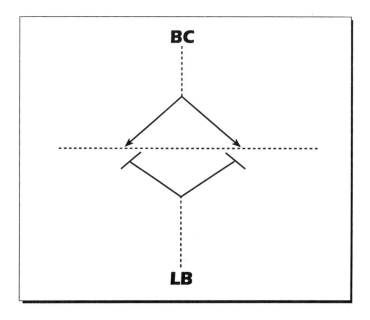

DRILL #46: SIDELINE TACKLING

Objective: To teach linebackers to utilize the sideline to help contain the ball carrier; to practice maintaining a proper spatial relationship with a ballcarrier; to practice proper tackling techniques.

Equipment Needed: A football.

Description: The drill involves three players—one acting as a quarterback, one serving as a ballcarrier, and one designated as a linebacker. The quarterback lines up on a hash mark, with the ballcarrier positioned approximately three yards directly behind him. The linebacker faces the quarterback, approximately 8 - 10 yards down field. On command from the coach, the quarterback can either pitch the ball immediately to the running back or run the option—both toward the sideline. The linebacker must immediately square up, read the play, contain it, and make the tackle.

Coaching Points:

- The drill can be run at half-speed initially before running it live.

- The linebacker should keep his body under control at all times.

- To prevent the ballcarrier from cutting back, the linebacker should maintain an inside-out relationship (i.e., approximately one yard to the strong side) with the ballcarrier.

- The linebacker should force the ballcarrier to the sideline.

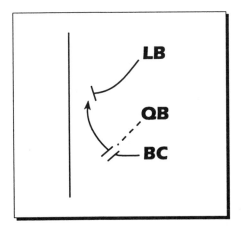

DRILL #47: CIRCLE ESCAPE

Objective: To develop the proper techniques and fundamentals of tackling, particularly gang tackling.

Equipment Needed: A football.

Description: A ballcarrier is located in the middle of a 12-to-15 foot (diameter) circle. The players on the perimeter are tacklers, set up in a good, ready position, with their feet moving and their eyes on the target. The ballcarrier either tries to run between two linebackers, or directly at a linebacker, in order to "escape" from the circle. If he attempts to go between two linebackers, the defenders on each side of the gap must close it. They then both tackle the ballcarrier. If he runs directly at a linebacker, the latter must meet him head-on, while the linebackers on each side must close in for a gang tackle. The linebacker who lets the ballcarrier "escape" replaces him in the middle of the circle.

Coaching Points:

•   The ballcarrier in the middle of the circle should perform the drill only three times if he does not "escape" sooner, because of the high level of contact involved in the drill.

•   Proper tackling fundamentals and techniques should be stressed.

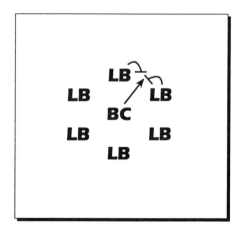

DRILL #48: MAT TACKLE

Objective: To teach proper tackling form; to provide the linebacker with the sensation of driving a ballcarrier to his back.

Equipment Needed: One blocking bag; one mat.

Description: A mat is positioned on the ground, and a bag is placed in front of the mat. The linebacker aligns directly in front of the ballcarrier. For the straight-on tackle, the ballcarrier aligns in front of the middle of the bag and comes forward in a straight line. The linebacker tackles him, driving him back onto the mat (over the bag). For the angle tackle, the ballcarrier starts at one end of the bag and comes forward at about a 45-degree angle. After the ballcarrier starts his move, the linebacker attacks him and drives him back onto the mat over the bag.

Coaching Points:

• The proper fundamentals and techniques of tackling should be stressed.

• Upon contact, the linebacker should keep his legs moving while driving the ballcarrier back onto the mat.

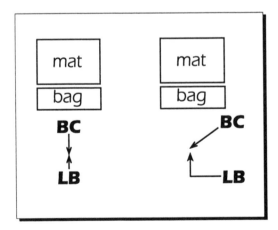

DRILL #49: GOAL-LINE TACKLE

Objective: To teach the proper techniques for making a tackle when a ballcarrier attempts to vault over a pile of linemen.

Equipment Needed: Four blocking bags; one mat.

Description: Three blocking bags are stacked in front of a mat to a height of about three and one-half feet. The coach stands on the mat with a blocking bag in his hands (preferably a light rectangular one) and then throws the bag over the pile in order to simulate a ball carrier. The linebacker, positioned on the other side of the pile, springs up and into the bag, and drives the bag back into the mat.

Coaching Points:

- The linebacker should keep his head up and his eyes focused on the center of the bag while springing up towards the bag.

- The linebacker should explode up and through the bag, and lock his arms around the bag upon contact.

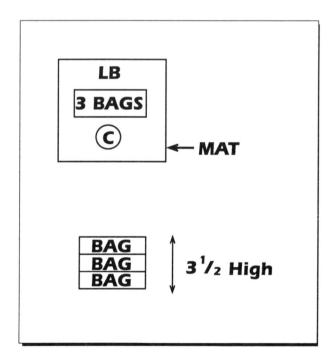

CHAPTER 4

SHEDDING BLOCKERS DRILLS

DRILL #50: DELIVER-A-BLOW

Objective: To enhance the ability of a linebacker to deliver a blow forcefully, to react to blockers at different angles, and to come off blocks properly.

Equipment Needed: A football.

Description: Three offensive blockers are aligned alongside each other about one and one half yards between each man. A ballcarrier is positioned about five yards behind the middle blocker, while the linebacker is aligned across from the middle blocker facing him. The coach points to one of the blockers which is a signal to the designated man to block the linebacker above the waist. The linebacker reacts by squaring up on the blocker and delivering a blow. After contact, both players recover to the starting positions as quickly as possible. The coach then points to another blocker and the drill continues. To conclude the drill, the coach raises his hand to one side. On this signal, the ballcarrier goes in that direction, while the blocker on that side fires out. The linebacker plays off the block and then makes the tackle.

Coaching Points:

- The linebacker should square up on the blocker before delivering a blow.

- Proper fundamentals and techniques of delivering a blow should be emphasized.

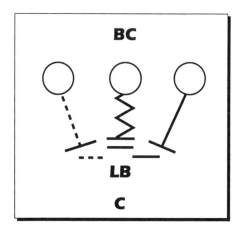

DRILL #51: BOUNCE

Objective: To enhance the ability of a linebacker to deliver a blow to a blocker; to improve the arm-leg synchronization involved in warding off a blocker.

Equipment Needed: None.

Description: Two offensive blockers assume a semi-upright position 12 to 18 inches apart, while the linebacker takes a "ready" position about two feet from the blockers. The blocker who is on the right steps toward the linebacker. The linebacker then delivers a blow to the blocker with the same shoulder and foot forward, steps back, then steps toward the other (left) blocker with the proper shoulder and foot forward, and finally steps back. This sequence should be repeated six times.

Coaching Points:

- Proper arm-leg synchronization in delivering a blow should be stressed.

- The linebacker should step back each time after delivering a blow.

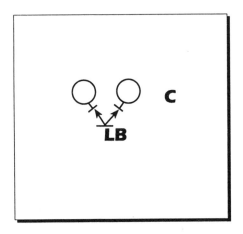

DRILL #52: HIT-SHUFFLE-HIT

Objective: To enhance the ability of a linebacker to deliver a blow to ward off (i.e., destroy) an offensive man's block.

Equipment Needed: None.

Description: The drill involves two players—an offensive blocker and a linebacker. The linebacker assumes a "ready" position, "hits" the blocker with his right shoulder, shuffles laterally to his right, and hits with his left shoulder, shuffles laterally to his left, and then hits with his right shoulder. This sequence should be repeated three times with each shoulder for a total of six blows.

Coaching Points:

•   Proper fundamentals of delivering a blow to a blocker should be emphasized.

•   Proper arm-leg synchronization while delivery a blow should be stressed.

•   Linebackers should not false-step while delivering a blow.

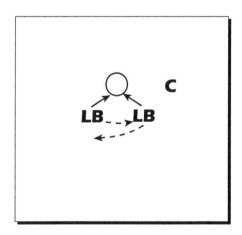

DRILL #53: HIT-HIT-HIT

Objective: To enhance the ability of a linebacker to deliver blow in order to destroy an offensive man's block.

Equipment Needed: None.

Description: The drill involves two players—an offensive blocker and a linebacker. The linebacker takes his proper alignment laterally, with both players in the "ready" position. The blocker steps toward the linebacker, who jab-steps and throws his forearm to destroy the block. The blocker steps back and comes again, while the linebacker recoils and uncoils again three times. Both men "bounce" up and back, with the linebacker practicing delivering a controlled blow to the chest of the blocker. The linebacker then repeats the drill three more times, while using the other shoulder (simulating that the block is coming from outside-in, whereas the other block was from inside-out). If the linebacker is using a staggered stance, he should not reverse the position of his feet. Rather, the linebacker should deliver the blow with the same shoulder and foot forward, especially when the blocker is coming from the outside-in.

Coaching Points:

- Proper fundamentals and techniques of delivering a blow to destroy a block should be stressed.

- Quickness and proper arm-leg synchronization should be emphasized.

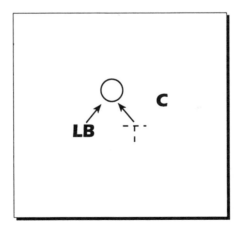

DRILL #54: PYRAMID

Objective: To enhance the ability of a linebacker to deliver a blow to a blocker; to practice using the proper arm-leg synchronization while delivering a blow.

Equipment Needed: None.

Description: Same as drill #51 (the bounce drill). The only differences are that three offensive blockers are used in this drill and that the coach stands behind the linebacker and indicates which blocker is to attack him. The linebacker starts from a "ready" position, jab-steps to meet the blocker with the proper shoulder and foot, and returns to the original position ready to ward off a blocker again. This sequence should be repeated six times.

Coaching Points:

• Proper arm-leg synchronization while delivering a blow should be stressed.

• The linebacker should recoil each time after delivering a blow.

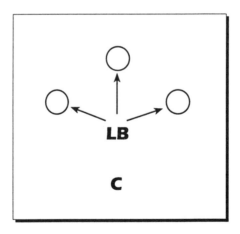

DRILL #55: MACHINE GUN

Objective: To enhance arm and leg coordination; to improve the ability of a linebacker to shed multiple blockers.

Equipment Needed: Four upright blocking dummies.

Description: Four upright dummies are set up inside a five-yard square forming an approximately three-yard box. The linebacker assumes a "ready" position a foot inside the front line of his box. Three or more blockers line up in a column a yard off the line outside the box. The coach controls the flow of blockers so that the linebacker must ward off and shed the blockers just as fast as the coach sends them. The linebacker tries to keep from being driven out of the box, and must ward off the blockers with his hands, knees, elbows, forearms, depending on how quickly the blockers come at him. If knocked down, the linebacker must get up immediately and keep fighting to shed each blocker as the coach continues to send blockers at him.

Coaching Points:

- Quickness and meeting blockers from the front should be stressed.

- The linebackers should not allow themselves to get spun around and turn their backs to the flow or direction of the blockers.

- Blockers should not clip from behind if the linebacker gets turned around.

- Piling on should be controlled by regulating the flow of blockers if the linebacker is knocked off his feet.

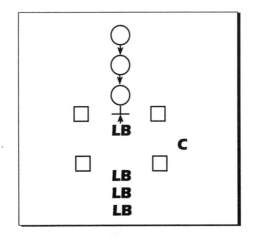

DRILL #56: BULL-IN-THE-RING SHED

Objective: To develop arm and leg coordination; to improve the ability of a linebacker to move his feet rapidly; to enhance the level of body balance involved in shedding a blocker.

Equipment Needed: None.

Description: The "bull" (linebacker) is positioned in the center of the circle, pumping his arms and legs, and moving in a counterclockwise direction slowly. The bull can point at the blocker he wants to attack him, the coach can indicate the blocker, or the blocker can come on his own from the rim and try to drive the linebacker out of the circle with a running shoulder block. The bull meets the blockers, one at a time, synchronizing the proper arm-leg movement and forcefully delivering a blow to the blocker. The linebacker should shed the blocker, using the techniques described previously, and continue to turn to meet another blocker. Four or five repetitions should be performed before replacing the linebacker in the middle.

Coaching Points:

- Quickness, proper arm-leg action, and shedding the blocker as quickly as possible should be stressed. The linebacker should not wrestle with the blocker.

- Forearm-shoulder lifts should be alternated so that the linebacker cannot favor his strong side and protect his weak side.

- Clipping from behind should not be allowed.

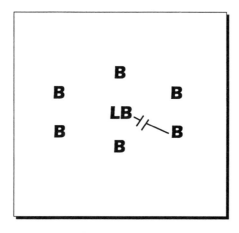

DRILL #57: AROUND-THE-CIRCLE HITTING

Objective: To enhance the ability of a linebacker from a semi-upright position to properly synchronize his arm-leg movements while delivering a blow to ward off a blocker and destroy the block.

Equipment Needed: None.

Description: Several blockers line up in a semi-upright stance in a circle facing clockwise. The linebacker is inside the circle in a semi-upright stance, working counterclockwise. The linebacker synchronizes throwing a forearm with the proper (right) foot forward as he meets limited resistance, pushes off, sprints to the next blocker, and repeats the technique around the circle. After each linebacker has a turn, the drill is repeated, with the linebacker going around the outside of the circle using the opposite (left) forearm and foot forward.

Coaching Points:

• Speed, quickness, and proper arm-leg synchronization should be emphasized.

DRILL #58: CONTROL AND REACT

Objective: To practice making an explosive defensive charge; to improve the ability of a linebacker to react to and ward off an offensive block.

Equipment Needed: None.

Description: The players pair up. One player serves as an offensive blocker (O), while the other player acts as the linebacker (LB). The linebacker assumes his proper defensive stance. The coach tells the linebackers what defensive alignment, type of charge, and type of protection against the block that they should employ. On command from the coach to begin the drill, the blocker attempts to block the linebacker. The linebacker reacts to the first movement of the blocker and counters the block with an aggressive hand shiver. Applying hand and arm pressure, the linebacker controls the blocker and puts himself in a proper position to locate the football. He then pursues the ballcarrier and makes the tackle.

Coaching Points:

- Emphasis should be placed on maintaining a proper defensive position at all times during the drill.

- The linebackers should be reminded to keep their heads from being extended past their shoulders while they are attempting to control the blocker.

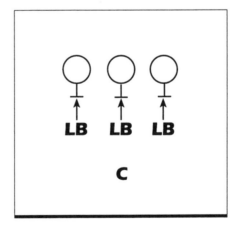

DRILL #59: HIT AND GO

Objective: To teach and practice the proper fundamentals and techniques for performing a hand shiver; to learn to control a blocker.

Equipment Needed: None

Description: The drill involves having the players pair up. One player serves as an offensive blocker (O), while the other acts as the linebacker (LB). The two players assume their proper stance, approximately four yards apart. On the command "go" from the coach (who is positioned behind the linebackers), the linebacker delivers a series of three, full-speed hand shivers against the blocker who initially is moving against the linebacker at half speed. As the drill progresses, the blocker moves at full speed. The linebacker eventually follows up his hand shivers with a slap step (i.e., the follow through with his opposite foot). The linebacker's ultimate goal is to gain separation from the blocker to the outside.

Coaching Points:

• Emphasis should be placed on having the linebackers keep their heads up during the drill and avoid overextending with their arms.

• Linebackers should maintain proper alignment and position at all times.

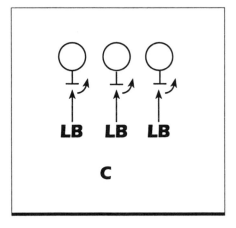

DRILL #60: DOUBLE SHIVER

Objective: To develop and practice the techniques involved in performing a hand shiver; to teach the skills to ward off a block; to improve reaction time.

Equipment Needed: None.

Description: The drill involves four players: two blockers and two linebackers. Having given the blockers (O) the snap count, the coach stands behind the blockers, facing the linebackers (LB). Responding to the coach's verbal count, the blockers fire out at the linebackers. The linebackers execute a hand shiver, control the blockers, and react to a hand signal given by the coach who points out whether they should perform a left or right pass rush.

Coaching Points:

* The proper techniques for performing a hand shiver should be emphasized—the heels of the hands should be driven forward and upward under the blocker's shoulder pads in an effort to straighten him up and neutralize his charge, the linebacker's elbows and wrists should be locked, and the linebacker should take short, choppy steps until he determines his direction of movement.

* The drill can be performed with a two-man sled (in lieu of the two blockers).

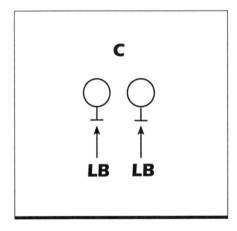

DRILL #61: SEVEN-MAN SLED

Objective: To develop and practice the proper techniques in performing a hand shiver; to improve the ability to exert maximum upper body power.

Equipment Needed: A seven-man sled.

Description: The drill involves having seven linebackers assume a proper defensive stance in front of the sled. On the coach's command, the seven linebackers (LB) fire out simultaneously and deliver a hand shiver against the sled. A secondary goal is to have the linebackers strike the sled so powerfully as to lift it off the ground.

Coaching Points:

• Maintaining a proper stance and using the correct techniques for a hand shiver should be emphasized.

• Exerting maximum force on the hand shiver should be encouraged.

• Variety can be added to the drill by having the linebackers line up initially to the left of the sled. On the coach's command, the first linebacker in line fires out against the first pad on the sled, pivots and moves to his right, and then fires out against the second pad—continuing on down the sled until he has struck every pad with a forceful hand shiver. As soon as the first linebacker moves to the second station on the sled, the next man in line starts the drill, and so on.

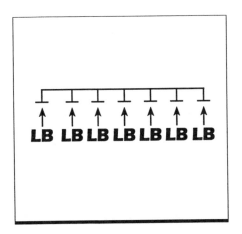

DRILL #62: GIVE A STEP

Objective: To teach the linebacker to give a step when a crack-back blocker approaches.

Equipment Needed: One football; two blocking dummies.

Description: The drill involves two players—a ballcarrier (BC) and a linebacker (LB). Two blocking dummies are placed at various locations along the path of the linebacker. When the linebacker gives ground and goes around the blocking dummy, he mirrors the ballcarrier while in pursuit. This action is designed to enable the linebacker to learn how to better avoid a crack-back block. After circumventing the blocking dummy, the linebacker continues to mirror the ballcarrier. When the ballcarrier turns up, the linebacker either tackles him or tags him (if the drill is being performed without pads).

Coaching Points:

- The linebacker should keep his shoulders square when going around a blocking dummy.

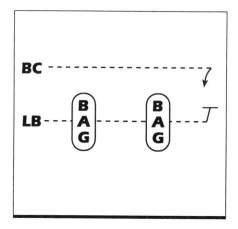

DRILL #63: CONTROL, PURSUE, AND TACKLE

Objective: To teach and develop the techniques involved in moving on the snap of the ball, controlling the blocker, locating the ball, and pursuing the ballcarrier.

Equipment Needed: One football.

Description: The drill involves three players: an offensive blocker (O), a ballcarrier (BC), and a linebacker (LB). Standing behind the linebacker, the coach flashes the starting count, the type of block, and the direction the ballcarrier should run. The coach verbally gives the linebacker the defensive alignment, the down, and the distance. Reacting to the coach's starting count, the blocker fires out and attempts to block the linebacker. The linebacker, on the other hand, hand shivers the blocker, attempts to control him, and then pursues and tags the ballcarrier.

Coaching Points:

- Assuming the proper defensive alignment and stance should be emphasized.

- Variety could be added to this drill by conducting it under "live" conditions and making the linebacker tackle the ballcarrier.

- The importance of linebackers using the proper angle of pursuit should be stressed.

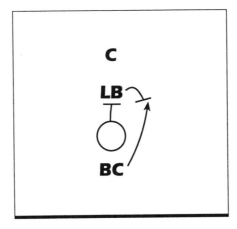

CHAPTER 5

PASS DEFENSE DRILLS

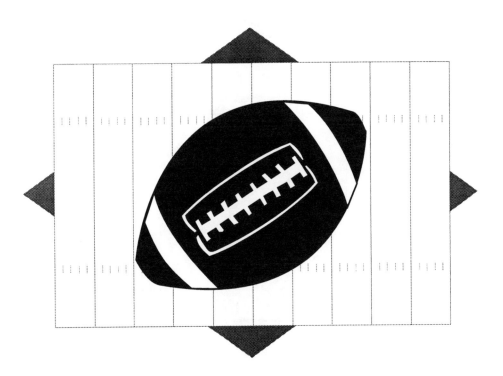

DRILL #64: ONE-HAND CATCH

Objective: To develop and improve a linebacker's ability to catch the football.

Equipment Needed: A football.

Description: The coach and a linebacker face each other at varying distances (seven to twelve yards). The ball is thrown to a point above the linebacker's head, where he must catch it with one hand.

Coaching Points:

• "Looking" the ball into the "catching" hand should be emphasized.

• A linebacker should "give" with his catching hand to cushion the ball's contact with his hand.

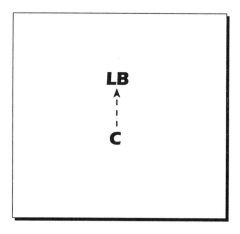

DRILL #65: TWO-HAND CATCH

Objective: To develop and improve a linebacker's ability to catch the football.

Equipment Needed: A football.

Description: The coach and linebacker face each other at varying distances between seven and 20 yards. The ball is thrown to the linebacker so that he must catch it with his hands in various positions.

Coaching Points:

- "Looking" the ball into the hands should be emphasized.

- A linebacker should "give" with his hands to cushion the ball's contact with his hands.

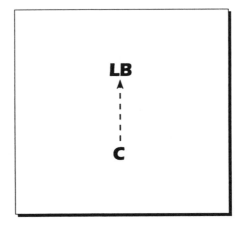

DRILL #66: STEP-FORWARD CATCH

Objective: To develop and improve a linebacker's ability to catch the football.

Equipment Needed: A football.

Description: The ball is thrown to the linebacker in the same manner as the two-hand catch, but the linebacker now comes one or two steps forward to catch the ball at the highest possible point.

Coaching Points:

- "Looking" the ball into the hands should be emphasized.

- When catching the ball, a linebacker should "give" with his hands to cushion the ball's contact with his hands.

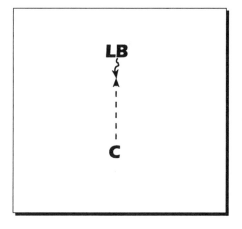

DRILL #67: LOOK

Objective: To develop and improve a linebacker's ability to catch the football.

Equipment Needed: A football.

Description: The linebacker stands with his back to the coach at a distance of about ten yards. On the coach's command, "look," the linebacker turns completely around to face the coach, and to catch the ball which the coach has thrown to him. The linebacker steps forward to catch the ball at the highest possible point.

Coaching Points:

- The linebacker should try to pick up the flight of the ball as soon as he turns around.

- "Looking" the ball into the hands should be emphasized.

- The linebacker should "give" with his hands to cushion the ball's contact with his hands.

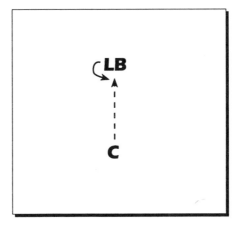

DRILL #68: CONCENTRATION

Objective: To develop and improve a linebacker's ability to catch the football.

Equipment Needed: A football.

Description: Two players are positioned in front of a linebacker. All of the players face the coach at a distance of approximately ten yards. As the ball is thrown, the two players wave their hands in front of the linebacker but do not touch the ball. Concentrating on the ball, the linebacker concentrates and catches the ball.

Coaching Points:

•   "Looking" the ball into the hands should be emphasized.

•   The linebacker should "give" with his hands to cushion the ball's contact with his hands.

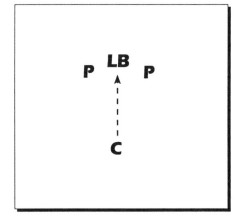

DRILL #69: ANGLE INTERCEPTION

Objective: To develop and improve a linebacker's ability to catch the football.

Equipment Needed: A football.

Description: The drill involves several linebackers at a time who form a semi-circle facing the coach. Some type of object is placed on the ground at a distance of about seven yards from the linebackers and ten yards from the coach. The linebackers are positioned beyond the object so that they must come forward at various angles to catch the ball. The coach signals which linebacker is "active." The designated linebacker then runs toward the marker. At that point, the ball is thrown, and the catch is made in front of the marker.

Coaching Points:

- "Looking" the ball into the hands should be emphasized.

- The linebacker should "give" with his hands to cushion the ball's contact with his hands.

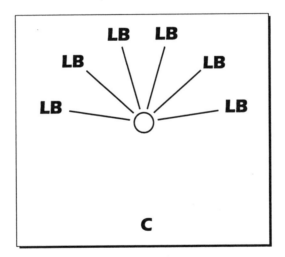

DRILL #70: LINEBACKER'S LEAP

Objective: To develop the skills needed for leaping into the air to catch the football.

Equipment Needed: None.

Description: The linebackers start on the five-yard line in a single column and sprint toward the goal posts, one at a time. First time through, the linebacker tries to touch the crossbar (ten feet from the ground) with his right hand; the second time, with his left hand; and the third time, with both hands. These actions are designed to simulate a linebacker leaping into the air to catch or defend against the high pass.

Coaching Points:

- The linebacker should focus on three factors—the gathering and leaping into the air without stopping, timing his take-off, and touching the crossbar.

- The linebacker should not grab the bar and/or attempt to swing on it.

- To add variety to the drill, the coach could have players stand under the bar and have them attempt to jump from a stationary position and touch the crossbar.

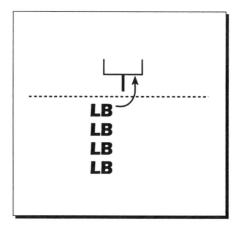

DRILL #71: MATCH-UP ZONE

Objective: To emphasize quick hands, concentration, and peripheral vision.

Equipment Needed: A football.

Description: The linebacker looks at the coach and assumes a position with his feet at approximately a 45-degree angle to the coach. The distance between them is approximately ten yards. On the coach's "look," the linebacker breaks to intercept the ball (pivots back to face the ball or just breaks), shouts "fire," and then sprints toward the coach for a distance of five yards.

Coaching Points:

•   The linebacker should try to pick up the flight of the ball as soon as he turns around.

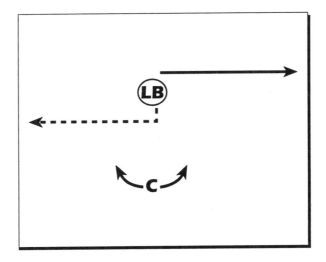

DRILL #72: SEMI-CIRCLE PERIPHERAL VISION

Objective: To emphasize quick hands, concentration, and peripheral vision.

Equipment Needed: Two footballs.

Description: Several players form a semicircle around a designated linebacker. The designated player and the first man in the semicircle both have footballs. As soon as the designated player passes the ball to the second man, the first player passes the ball to him. This pattern continues around the semicircle and then back to the starting point.

Coaching Points:

- "Looking" the ball into the hands should be emphasized.

- The linebacker should "give" with his hands to cushion the ball's contact with his hands.

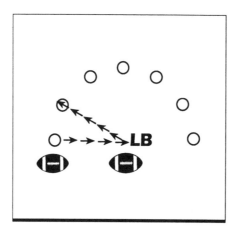

DRILL #73: TERMINAL MIRROR

Objective: To teach the linebacker his proper position in relation to a receiver in his zone; to have him anticipate making an interception.

Equipment Needed: A football.

Description: A receiver is positioned at an angle 20 yards from the coach. The linebacker positions himself between the receiver and the coach so that he can see both of them (as diagrammed). The coach signals to the receiver whether the ball will be thrown on the receiver's break or the coach's look. The linebacker reacts to the first movement of either the coach or the receiver and moves to make the interception. When the ball is caught by the linebacker, he shouts "fire" and sprints forward to the coach at full speed for five yards.

Coaching Points:

- "Looking" the ball into the hands should be emphasized.

- The linebacker should "give" with his hands to cushion the ball's contact with his hands.

- The coach should instruct the linebacker to go through the receiver to make the interception.

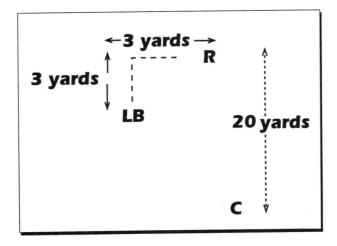

DRILL #74: LATERAL RETREAT MIRROR

Objective: To teach the linebacker his proper position in relation to a receiver in his zone; to have him anticipate making an interception; to teach the linebacker to retreat to his zone.

Equipment Needed: A football.

Description: The procedure is the same as for the terminal mirror drill, except that the linebacker aligns himself seven yards from the coach and runs laterally back to the terminal position.

Coaching Points:

• "Looking" the ball into the hands should be emphasized.

• The linebacker should "give" with his hands to cushion the ball's contact with his hands.

• The coach should instruct the linebacker to go through the receiver to make the interception.

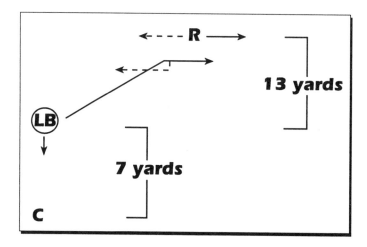

DRILL #75: LATERAL RETREAT-TO-THE-PATTERN

Objective: To develop the linebacker's ability to retreat to an area, to then read the offensive pattern and the ball, and to make an interception.

Equipment Needed: A football.

Description: The coach and the linebacker line up as they did in the lateral retreat mirror drill, while the receiver is positioned about eight to ten yards outside the linebacker. On command, the receiver runs straight down the field about 12 to 15 yards and breaks in or out. The coach throws the ball on the receiver's break. The linebacker retreats to his terminal position, makes the interception, shouts "fire," and sprints five yards forward at full speed.

Coaching Points:

• "Looking" the ball into the hands should be emphasized.

• The linebacker should "give" with his hands to cushion the ball's contact with his hands.

• The coach should instruct the linebacker to go through the receiver to make the interception.

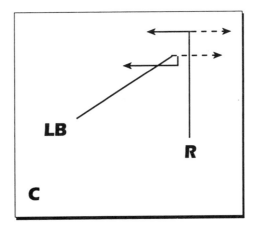

DRILL #76: TERMINAL BACK PEDAL

Objective: To learn to back pedal properly and to break on the ball at a proper angle to make the interception.

Equipment Needed: A football; two blocking bags.

Description: Two bags are positioned upright approximately 14 yards apart and 20 yards from the coach. A linebacker lines up three yards in front of the bags, midway between the two bags, facing the coach. On a signal from the coach, the linebacker back pedals until the coach looks at one of the bags. When the coach looks, the linebacker turns his shoulders and sprints at an angle to make the interception in front of the bag. After the ball is caught, the linebacker shouts "fire" and sprints forward for five yards.

Coaching Points:

•   "Looking" the ball into the hands should be emphasized.

•   The linebacker should "give" with his hands to cushion the ball's contact with his hands.

•   The coach should instruct the linebackers to break on the ball at a proper angle to make the interception.

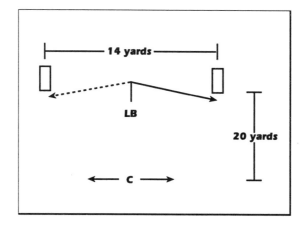

DRILL #77: LATERAL RETREAT AND BACK PEDAL

Objective: To teach the linebacker his proper position in relation to a receiver in his zone; to have him anticipate making an interception; to teach the linebacker to retreat to his zone.

Equipment Needed: A football; two blocking bags.

Description: The bags are placed in the same position as in the terminal back pedal drill. The coach aligns in front of one of the bags at a distance of 20 yards, while the linebacker is seven yards in front of the coach. On a signal, the linebacker runs laterally to the terminal spot (12 yards deep and midway between the bags) and from that point everything is the same as in the terminal back pedal drill.

Coaching Points:

- "Looking" the ball into the hands should be emphasized.

- The linebacker should "give" with his hands to cushion the ball's contact with his hands.

- The coach should instruct the linebackers to break on the ball at a proper angle to make the interception.

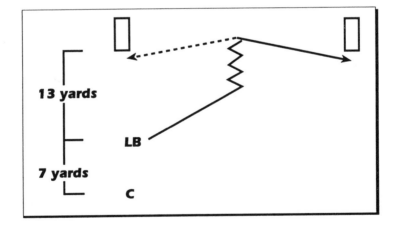

DRILL #78: TWO-MAN TIP

Objective: To ensure that the linebacker continues to pursue the ball until it hits the ground.

Equipment Needed: A football; two blocking bags.

Description: Two bags are positioned upright, approximately 18 yards apart. The coach stands midway between the bags, about 20 yards away. Two linebackers line up alongside each other and face the coach—approximately seven yards from him. On a signal, each linebacker retreats to the bag on his side. The ball is then thrown to one of the linebackers when he reaches the bag. That linebacker then tips the ball into the air. The other linebacker sprints to the ball and catches it at the highest possible point. Both linebackers then sprint full speed back to the coach.

Coaching Points:

•   The linebacker should watch the ball (not the player who tipped the ball).

•   The linebacker should use proper two-hand catching techniques.

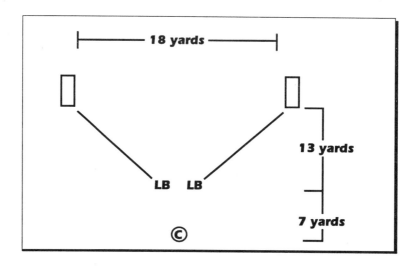

DRILL #79: COMBAT TIP DRILL

Objective: To develop the skills needed for competing for a deflected ball in flight.

Equipment Needed: A football; two blocking bags.

Description: Same as the two-man tip drill, but two players approach the tipper and compete to intercept the deflected ball, thereby simulating a receiver and a defender fighting to catch the football.

Coaching Points:

• Defenders should watch the ball (not their opponent).

• Players may use their bodies to ward off each other legally while attempting to catch the ball, but they should not push or shove illegally.

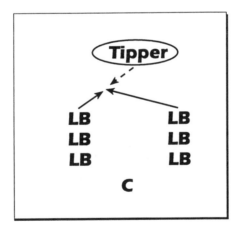

DRILL #80: ONE-ON-ONE COVERAGE

Objective: To enhance the ability of a linebacker to cover a receiver man-for-man, both cautiously and aggressively.

Equipment Needed: None.

Description: The linebacker covers a receiver all over the field, using either cautious or aggressive man-for-man techniques.

Coaching Points:

- Proper pass coverage and catching fundamentals and techniques should be stressed.

- Variety can be incorporated into the drill by having a coach throw a pass to the receiver, thereby creating a "live" (go-for-the -ball) coverage situation.

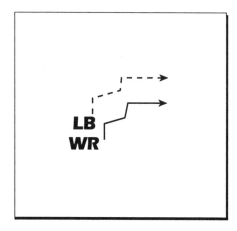

DRILL #81: ZONE DRILL

Objective: To define the five underneath pass zones in relation to the ball and the field; to enhance the ability of the linebackers to retreat to those areas.

Equipment Needed: A football.

Description: The coach stands in different positions on the field holding a ball. When everyone is ready, he drops straight back, and the linebackers retreat to their proper zones. On the coach's signal, they all stop. Each linebacker's position is checked, and then the ball is moved to another spot on the field.

Coaching Points:

- The coach should check to make sure each linebacker has taken a proper pass drop before moving the ball to another spot on the field.

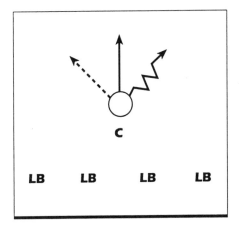

DRILL #82: SKELETON PASS DRILL

Objective: To coordinate the pass defense against the opponent's anticipated pass routes.

Equipment Needed: A football.

Description: All of a team's defensive personnel, except the tackles, defend against a quarterback, the center, and all eligible receivers. The offensive players run pass patterns at different positions, in sequence, and against predetermined defenses. The defenders read the play and react accordingly.

Coaching Points:

* The coach should instruct each linebacker to retreat to his proper zone.

* Proper pass coverage and catching fundamentals and techniques should be emphasized.

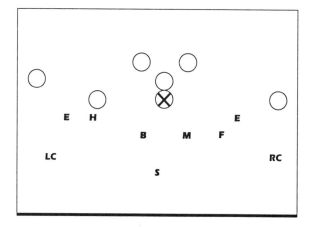

DRILL #83: GOAL-LINE ZONE PASS DEFENSE

Objective: To teach linebacker assignments and techniques according to the action of the ball in playing goal-line, zone-pass defense.

Equipment Needed: A football.

Description: Holding a ball, the coach stands inside the ten-yard line at different positions on the field. When everyone is ready, the coach drops straight back or sprints to either side, while the linebackers retreat to their proper zones. On the coach's signal, they stop. Each linebacker's position is checked; the ball is then moved to another spot on the field.

Coaching Points:

- The coach should check to make sure each linebacker has taken a proper pass drop before moving the ball to another spot on the field.

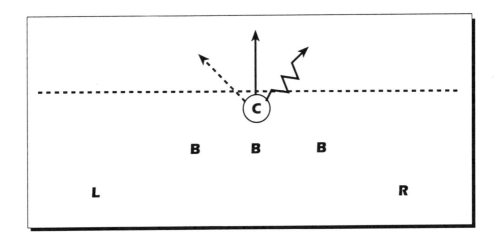

DRILL #84: GOAL-LINE PASS SKELETON

Objective: To defend against anticipated goal-line passes in order to give the linebackers a feel for playing pass defense inside the ten-yard line.

Equipment Needed: A football.

Description: Offensive backs and receivers run patterns against those linebackers involved in goal-line pass coverage. The plays are run from the ten-yard line to the goal-line, in sequence, off cards, and against predetermined defenses.

Coaching Points:

- Each linebacker should be instructed to retreat to his proper zone.

- Proper pass coverage and catching fundamentals and techniques should be stressed.

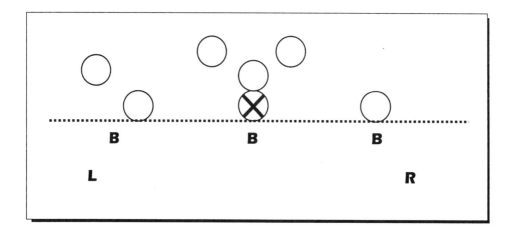

CHAPTER 6

RUN DEFENSE DRILLS

DRILL #85: HALF-LINE KEY

Objective: To teach outside linebackers the proper way to react to the various blocks that they will encounter on a running play; to enhance the ability of a linebacker to make a tackle once he has warded off a blocker.

Equipment Needed: None.

Description: An offensive guard, tackle, tight end, and running back align in their normal positions. An outside linebacker sets up in his normal position with the coach behind him. The coach points out the blocking scheme to the offensive players. On the coach's command, the offensive players execute the designated blocking pattern. The linebacker plays off the block and makes the proper reaction.

Coaching Points:

•   The proper fundamentals and techniques for delivering a blow should be stressed.

•   Variety can be added to the drill by having the running back go "live" off his teammate's block and by having the defender then attempt to tackle him.

•   If the drill is conducted with a ballcarrier running "live," the proper fundamentals and techniques for tackling should be emphasized.

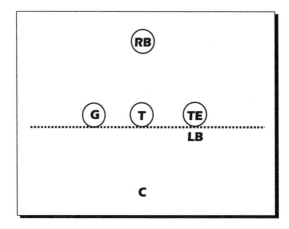

DRILL #86: INSIDE KEY

Objective: To teach inside linebackers and defensive tackles the proper reaction to the various inside plays that they will encounter.

Equipment Needed: None.

Description: All interior offensive linemen and all the offensive backs run plays against the two defensive tackles (DT) and the inside linebackers (LB). The plays are run off cards, in sequence, and against predetermined defenses. The defenders ward off the blocks, react to the play, and move to the ballcarrier. Initially, the drill can be performed at a controlled speed. Subsequently, it should be conducted "live."

Coaching Points:

- The proper fundamentals and techniques for delivering a blow should be stressed.

- The proper fundamentals and techniques for tackling should be emphasized.

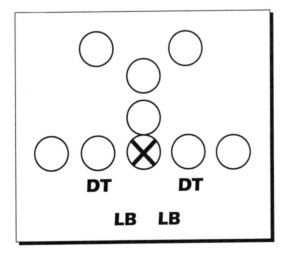

DRILL #87: OUTSIDE PLAY

Objective: To teach the proper read, reaction, and pursuit to the various outside plays that an opponent runs.

Equipment Needed: None.

Description: An offensive team runs outside plays against a complete defensive team. The plays are run off cards, in sequence, from different positions on the field, and against predetermined defenses. The defense wards off the blockers, reacts to the play, and moves to the ballcarrier. Initially, the drill can be conducted at a controlled speed. Subsequently, it should be conducted "live."

Coaching Points:

- The proper fundamentals and techniques for delivering a blow should be stressed.

- The proper fundamentals and techniques for tackling should be emphasized.

- The importance of the linebackers using the proper angle of pursuit should be stressed.

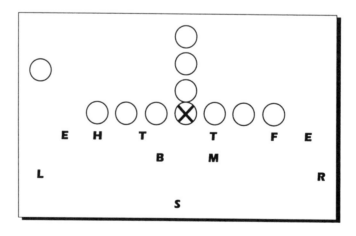

DRILL #88: GOAL-LINE CORNER RUN SUPPORT

Objective: To teach an outside linebacker the proper run support techniques against outside runs in a goal-line situation.

Equipment Needed: A football.

Description: Outside plays are run at a linebacker by an offensive backfield and one-half of an offensive line. The plays are run in sequence and off cards. The linebacker wards off the blockers, reacts to the play, and moves to the ball.

Coaching Points:

•   The proper fundamentals and techniques for delivering a blow should be emphasized.

•   The proper fundamentals and techniques for tackling should be stressed.

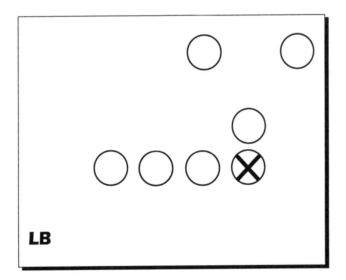

DRILL #89: GOAL-LINE TEAM

Objective: To have the defensive team react as a unit to the anticipated goal-line plays.

Equipment Needed: A football.

Description: An offensive team runs goal-line plays against the complete defense. The plays are run off cards, in sequence, from different positions on the field, and against predetermined defenses. The defenders ward off the blockers, react to the play, and move to the ball. Initially, the drill can be performed at a controlled speed. Subsequently, it should be conducted "live."

Coaching Points:

•   The proper fundamentals and techniques for delivering a blow should be stressed.

•   The proper fundamentals and techniques for tackling should be emphasized.

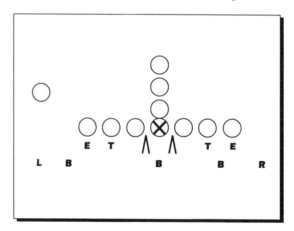

DRILL #90: READ AND REACT

Objective: To develop the linebacker's ability to read a block, fight pressure, and react against two blockers.

Equipment Needed: None.

Description: Initially, five offensive men (O) line up with their inside knees on the ground or lined-up on their hands and knees, shoulder-to-shoulder with each other. Four linebackers (LB) line up in the gap opposite the offensive players. The coach stands behind the offensive players and signals the linebackers when to move. On command, the linebackers explode into the gap with their shoulders. As contact is made, each linebacker extends his legs straight and performs a forceful hand shiver. Upon contact, the linebacker brings his feet up under him and moves them hard and fast in short choppy steps, while assuming a position ready to react to the situation. After the linebackers get the feeling of exploding into the gap, the drill is then run live. The blockers assume their normal offensive stance and, on signal, attempt to block the linebackers. The linebackers ward off the block and react accordingly.

Coaching Points:

- Having the linebackers make their first move forward when exploding should be emphasized.

- Maintaining proper body position at all times should be stressed.

- Variety can be added to the "live" phase of the drill by having the linebackers react to hand signals given by the coach once contact is made with the blockers.

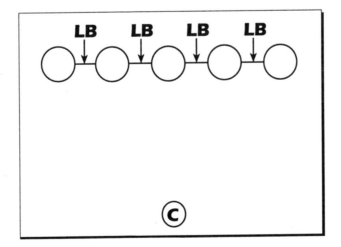

DRILL #91: THUD

Objective: To present game situations to the linebackers in order to enable them to condition themselves to the tempo of the game.

Equipment Needed: A football.

Description: This practice period involves an entire offensive and defensive team. The plays are run off cards, in sequence, from different positions on the field, and against predetermined defenses. The down and distance is called out for every play, and the ball is moved down the field. The plays are run quickly, and everyone must hustle in and out of the huddle. The blocking is conducted full speed, but the ballcarrier is not taken to the ground. Special situations, such as "get the ball back" defense and the "two minutes to go" defense, are practiced during this period. One sequence usually comprises ten to fourteen plays.

Coaching Points:

* The proper fundamentals and techniques for delivering a blow should be emphasized.

* The proper fundamentals and techniques for tackling should be stressed.

* The importance of the linebackers using the proper angle of pursuit should be stressed.

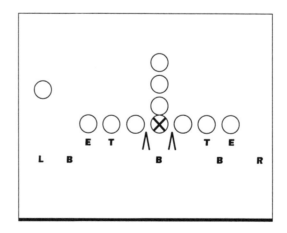

DRILL #92: EYE OPENER

Objective: To teach maintaining proper leverage on the ballcarrier, shedding the blocker, and tackling.

Equipment Needed: Four or five upright blocking dummies; a football.

Description: Upright dummies are placed on a straight line, with approximately five feet between each dummy. The linebacker is in a "ready" position behind one of the dummies, across from a blocker (O). A ballcarrier (BC) is lined up three yards behind the blocker. The blocker tells the ballcarrier which hole he is going to lead him through. The ballcarrier must go into that hole. The coach tosses the football to the ballcarrier, who follows his blocker. The linebacker meets the blocker in the hole, sheds him, and makes the tackle from an inside-out position, driving his head across and in front of the ballcarrier.

Coaching Points:

- To add variety to the drill, the ballcarrier may be allowed to either run directly into the "designated" hole or to fake once and go through the next hole.

- The linebacker should work from both the left side and the right side.

- Using proper leverage, shedding the blocker, and adhering to proper tackling fundamentals should be stressed.

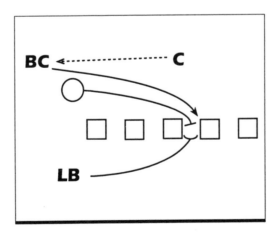

CHAPTER 7

FUMBLE RECOVERY DRILLS

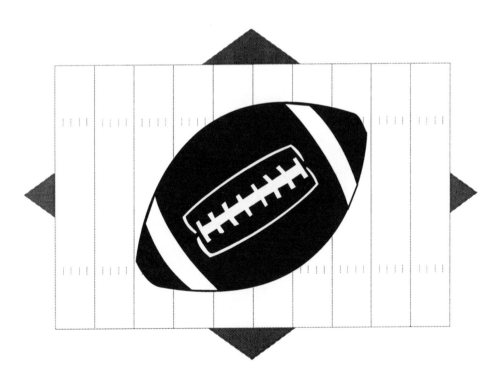

DRILL #93: FUMBLE FORM RECOVERY

Objective: To teach linebackers the proper method of falling on a loose football.

Equipment Needed: A football.

Description: A ball is placed three to four yards in front of a linebacker. On command from a coach, the linebacker dives forward and reaches out to the ball. On contact, the linebacker pulls the ball to his stomach and curls around the ball, lying on his side to protect himself.

Coaching Points:

•   Variety and competition can be added to the drill by using one ball per two (or more) lines and having two (or more) players go for a recovery simultaneously.

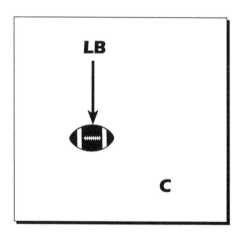

DRILL #94: COMPETITIVE FUMBLE RECOVERY

Objective: To teach linebackers to fight for a loose ball.

Equipment Needed: A football.

Description: Two linebackers line up alongside each other. On command from the coach, the linebackers fall forward, touch their chests to the ground, scramble after a ball that has been thrown between them and attempt to recover the ball.

Coaching Points:

• The linebacker should be required to pull the ball to his stomach on contact and curl around it.

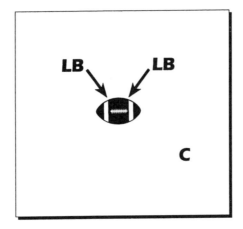

DRILL #95: REACT AND CATCH

Objective: To practice reacting to the snap of the football; to develop hand coordination and quickness; to enhance the ability of a linebacker to recover a fumble.

Equipment Needed: One (Nerf) football; two tennis balls.

Description: The drill involves two players, a coach, and someone to assimilate a snap. As the ball is snapped, the players' eyes focus on the tennis balls that are being held by the coach who is positioned three yards from the football. The coach has his arms out with his body forming a "T." Players react to the dropping of the tennis ball by the coach and try to catch the ball before it hits the ground a second time. After all players go a depth of three yards from the coach, the coach can move back to four yards, etc. A depth of five to six yards from the coach is considered especially challenging. The coach should be particularly alert once the competitive level of the drill is increased and players start diving for the tennis balls.

Coaching Points:

• Once the linebackers become proficient at reacting to and going for the tennis balls, the coach could switch to using two actual footballs.

• The key is to focus on reacting to the snap of the ball and on moving quickly to the falling tennis ball.

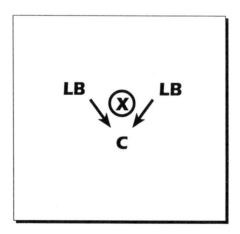

CHAPTER 8

PASS RUSHING DRILLS

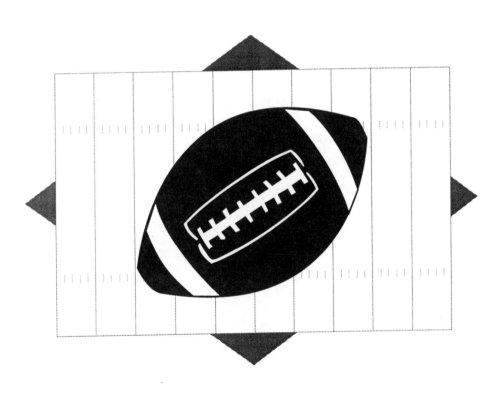

DRILL #96: OUTSIDE LINEBACKER TAKEOFF

Objective: To teach and practice the techniques involved with having the outside linebackers rush the passer.

Equipment Needed: A football; three cones or blocking dummies.

Description: The three cones are placed (as diagrammed) to represent the positions normally occupied by the tight end, the offensive tackle on the other side, and the fullback. The two linebackers line up outside the two cones placed on the yard line. On a signal by the coach, the linebackers (LB) rush across the line, staying low and aiming for a point approximately four yards deep behind the offensive center where the coach (C) stands in this drill. This drill can be performed live or without pads.

Coaching Points:

- If the drill is conducted against actual blockers, the linebackers should be reminded about the various steps involved in controlling blockers: grab the blocker at the shoulder; keep in mind that a blocker's butt is the source of his power; attempt to jerk the blocker forward or sideways; use the swim technique (bring their arm over the blocker's); execute a proper rip-up technique—bringing their hands from the outside to the inside and then up; counter the momentum of the blocker—get the blocker moving in one direction, then execute a move in the opposite direction; and reverse their rush angle from time to time (i.e., inside to outside, outside to inside, etc.).

- Linebackers rushing from the left (at a right-handed passer) should aim at the passer's arm for pressure and containment; those linebackers rushing from the right should aim for the passer's shoulders.

- The importance of having outside linebackers who are rushing to keep moving should be emphasized.

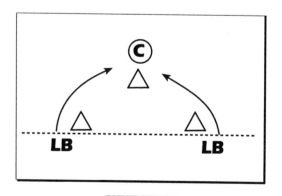

DRILL #97: REACT AND GO

Objective: To enhance the ability of a linebacker to react to ball movement, thereby improving his pass rushing skills.

Equipment Needed: A football; two cones or blocking dummies.

Description: The drill involves the coach and four players. Representing interior offensive linemen, two cones (or blocking dummies) are set up five yards apart on a yard line. Standing between the cones, the coach snaps the ball to an individual who is serving as a quarterback (QB). On movement of the ball, the three linebackers (LB) sprint low and hard across the line of scrimmage and converge on the quarterback at six yards.

Coaching Points:

- The coach should use various kinds of cadence before snapping the ball in order to get the linebackers used to reacting to the ball, as opposed to the "quarterback's" voice inflections. If necessary, a manager or an injured player can snap the ball.

- The coach should remind the linebackers that their first priority is to key the football and sprint six yards.

- After each repetition, the players should switch sides so they can attack from both sides.

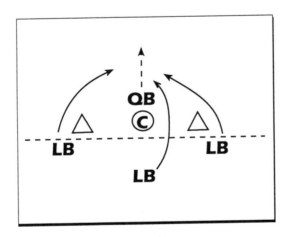

DRILL #98: IN-YOUR-FACE PASS RUSH

Objective: To enable linebackers to learn and practice the basic fundamentals and techniques involved in a bull rush (power pass rush).

Equipment Needed: None.

Description: The drill involves having the linebackers split up into two lines facing each other approximately one yard apart. One line is designated as blockers (O), while the other line serves as pass rushers (LB). On command from the coach, the first linebacker in line accelerates across the area in front of the offensive blockers, and explodes into the first player in the other line (the blocker). Using leverage, each linebacker drives his hands up through the armpits of the blocker he is facing. Defending his "turf," the blocker attempts to prevent the linebacker from advancing. Contact continues for a predetermined time (e.g., 3-5 seconds) until the coach blows his whistle. After a set number of repetitions, the players switch roles.

Coaching Points:

- The coach should make sure all players bull rush the same direction so that collisions are avoided.

- The drill should first be performed at a controlled speed and then, subsequently, at full speed once the basic movement mechanics have been mastered.

- The coach should emphasize the need for an explosive blow (strike) by the linebacker rather than a push.

- The first step by the linebacker should be with his inside foot.

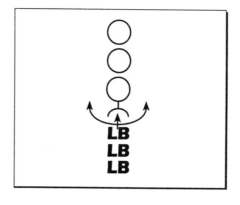

DRILL #99: BACK FOOT CARIOKA MOVE

Objective: To teach a method to cut the edge on a pass rush.

Equipment Needed: None.

Description: The drill involves having the linebackers (LB) pair up and position themselves so that each linebacker is aligned to the side of the offensive player (O). A linebacker's hands should be on the shoulder (grabbing the jersey) of the offensive player. On the command from the coach, the linebacker should pull down on the blocker's shoulder and at the same time take his inside foot and use a carioca move to get his hips beyond the blocker. The linebacker should then accelerate to the quarterback.

Coaching Points:

- The linebacker should be should be in a leverage position to start the drill.

- Once the drill begins, the linebacker should pull down on the shoulder of the offensive player.

- All linebackers should use their back feet when performing a carioca movement (no false steps).

- Once past the individual attempting to block him, the linebacker should accelerate to the quarterback.

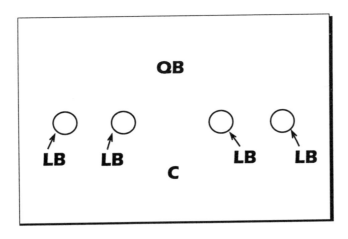

DRILL #100: PASS RUSH LANES

Objective: To develop the ability to stay in pass rush lanes.

Equipment Needed: None.

Description: Five offensive players and five defensive players are aligned in their proper lanes. One of the five linebackers is designated as "live." On the cadence (used by the offense), the "live" linebacker will execute a pass rush move and attempt to drive to the quarterback. The quarterback is in a shot-gun position. A coach should move from left to right on defense to determine who is "live." After a linebacker goes "live," he is replaced by another linebacker.

Coaching Points:

- Linebackers should be taught lane responsibility and should develop a "feel" about the actual distance to the quarterback.

- The designated pass rusher should rigorously rush the passer.

- All five linebackers should key and move forward on the snap of the ball.

- All linebackers should step north on the snap.

- A standup dummy should never be used as the simulated quarterback in this drill because offensive players may be knocked back into it causing injury. A more appropriate alternative would be to use a manager.

- No pushing should be allowed. A proper pass rush move should be used *every* time.

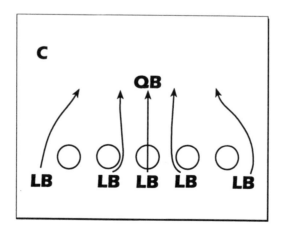

DRILL #101: LOCK, LIFT, AND SPIN

Objective: To develop the ability to use leverage; to practice the spin technique; to improve a linebacker's ability to shed a blocker.

Equipment Needed: None.

Description: The drill involves dividing the linebackers into two groups. One group acts as offensive blockers (O), while the other group serves as pass rushers (LB). The drill begins by having the players pair up and line up facing opposite directions on a yardage line, next to each other, hip to hip. On command from the coach (C), the defensive player dips his underarm and using leverage, explodes into the blocker in an attempt to dislodge him off the yardage line. Simultaneously, the blocker uses his hands and his body in an attempt to prevent any movement by the linebacker across the yardage line. After a predetermined number of repetitions, the players switch roles.

Coaching Points:

- The coach should emphasize the proper techniques for applying leverage.

- The drill continues full speed until the coach blows his whistle. Each player should go full tilt until he hears the whistle.

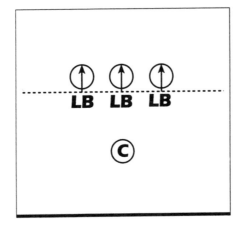

About the Authors

Jerry Sandusky

Jerry Sandusky is the assistant head coach, defensive coordinator, and inside linebackers coach at Penn State University. Credited with developing several of the most outstanding linebackers in the history of the NFL—Jack Hamm, Shane Conlon, Matt Millen, and Greg Buttle, among others, Sandusky is the architect of one of the most renowned and successful college defenses in the country. The success his disciples have experienced in the NFL has earned Penn State the title of "Linebacker U." Since joining Joe Paterno's Nittany Lion's staff in 1969, Penn State has appeared in 25 bowl games. Sandusky is widely regarded as one of the most respected and knowledgeable football coaches in America.

Cedric X. Bryant

Cedric X. Bryant., Ph.D., FACSM, serves as the director of sports medicine at StairMaster Sports/Medical Products, L.P. in Kirkland, Washington. Prior to assuming his present position, Dr. Bryant served on the exercise science faculties of the United States Military Academy at West Point, Penn State University, and Arizona State University. He is a fellow of ACSM and an associate editor of the *ACSM Guidelines for Exercise Testing and Prescription* (fifth edition). He is the author of numerous books and articles on health and fitness.